AF454099

© 2022 by ADISAN Publishing AB, Sweden

No part of this publication may be reproduced, stored in a retrieval system, or transmitted in any form or by any means, electronic, mechanical, photocopying, recording, scanning, or otherwise as permitted under section 107 and 108 of the 1976 United States Copyright Act, without the prior permission of the Publisher.

Pictures used in the book, unless otherwise stated are purchased as per Canva Pro Content Licenses agreement.

Limit of Liability/ Disclaimer of Warranty: The publisher and the author make no representations or warranties concerning the accuracy or completeness of this work's content and expressly. Neither the Publisher nor the author shall be liable for damages arising here.

Giant's Causeway, Scotland

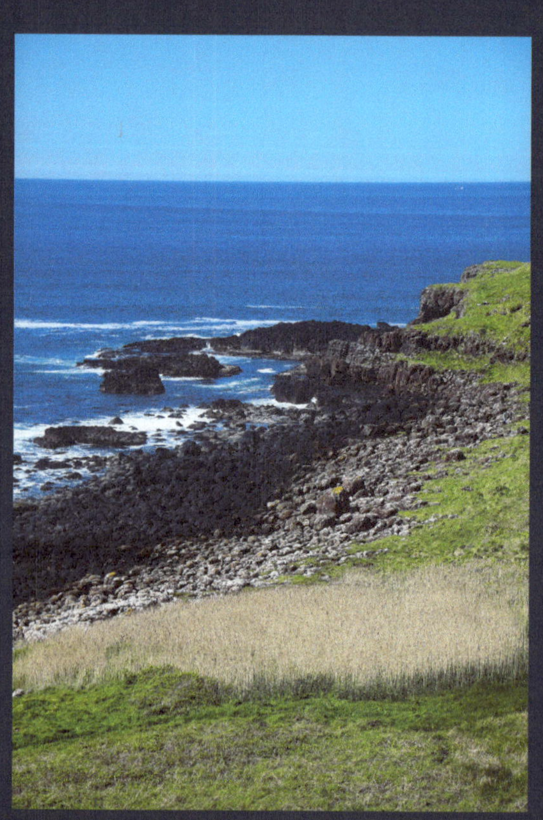

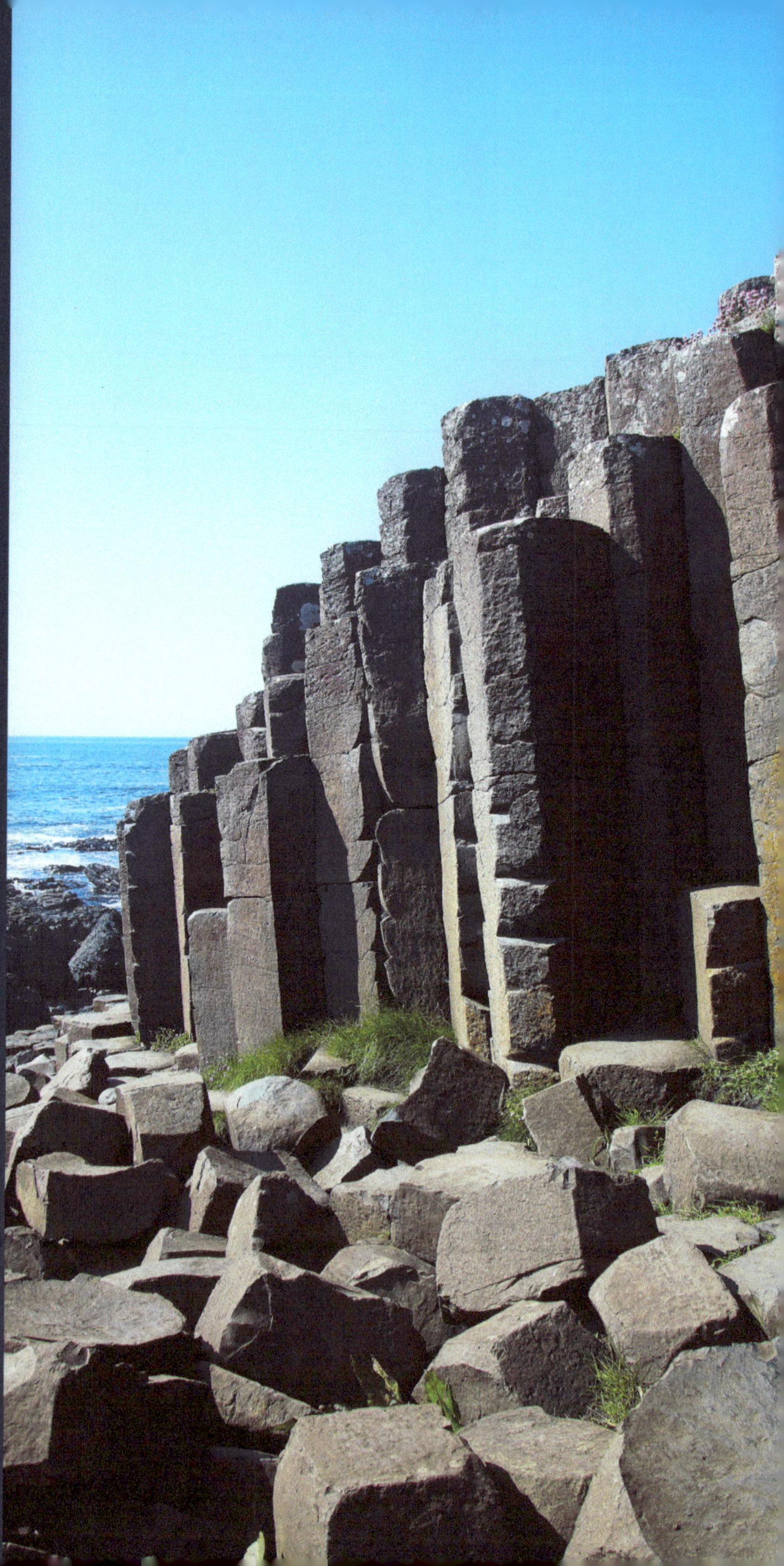

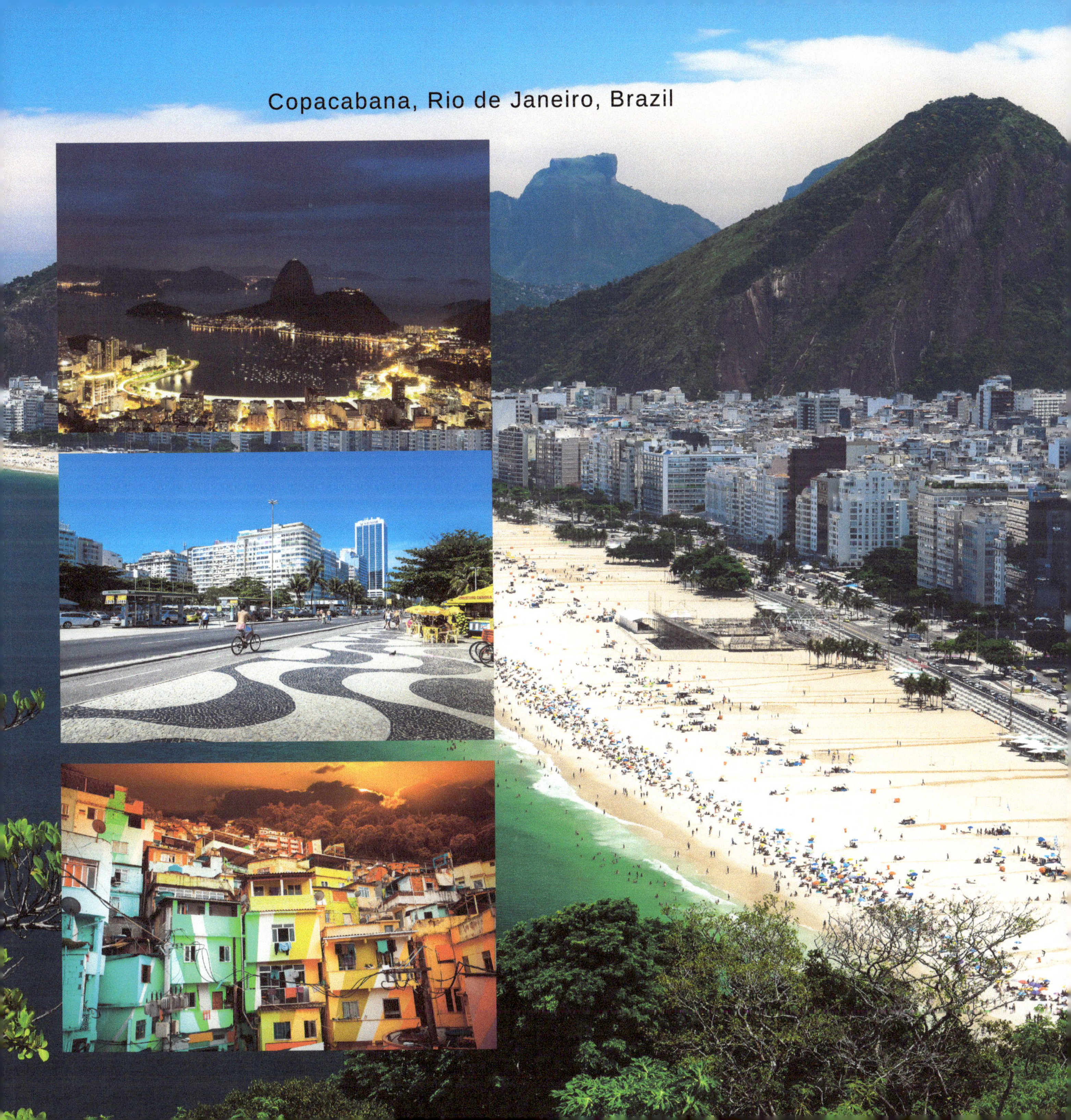
Copacabana, Rio de Janeiro, Brazil

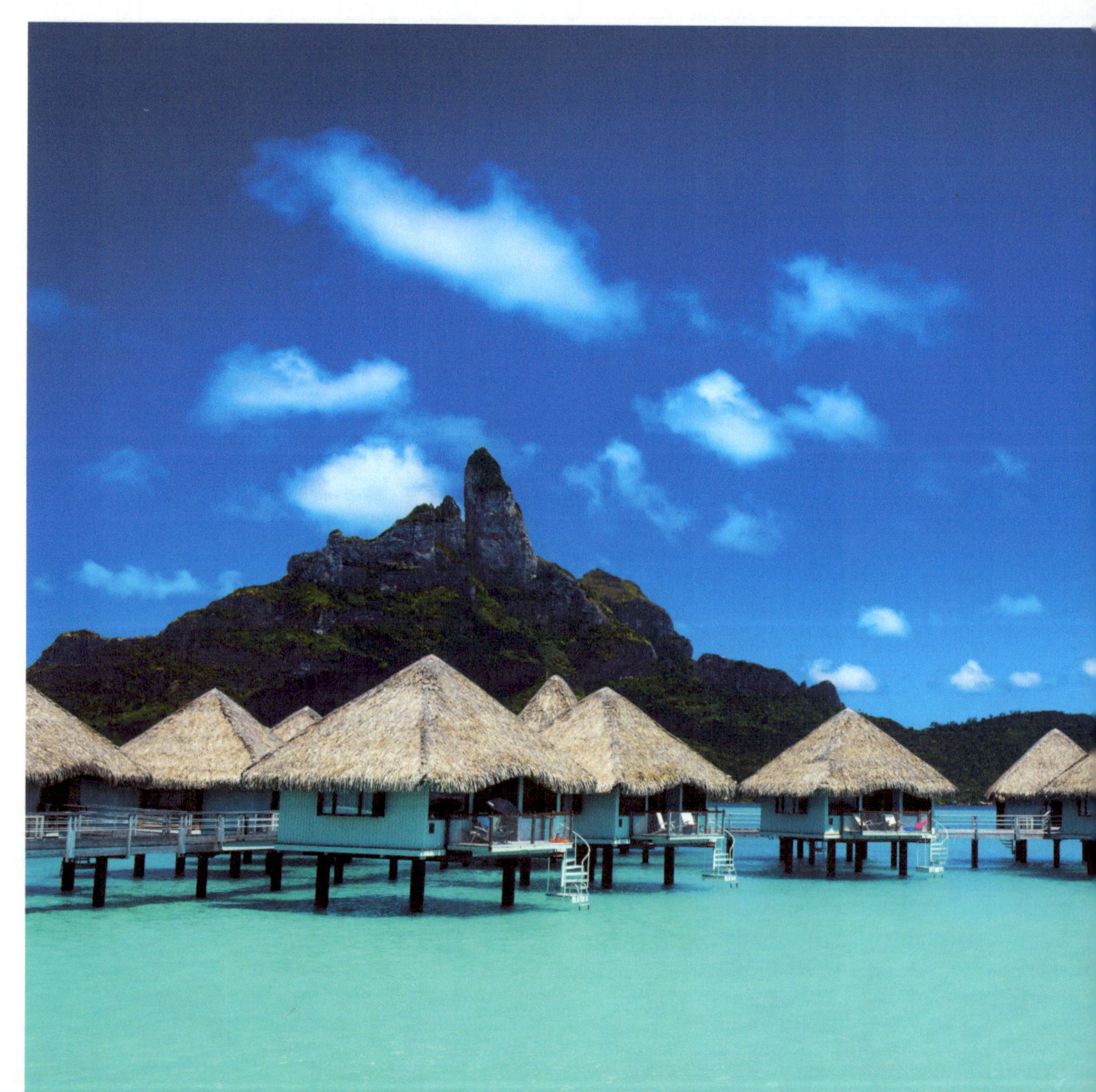

Matira Beach,
Bora Bora

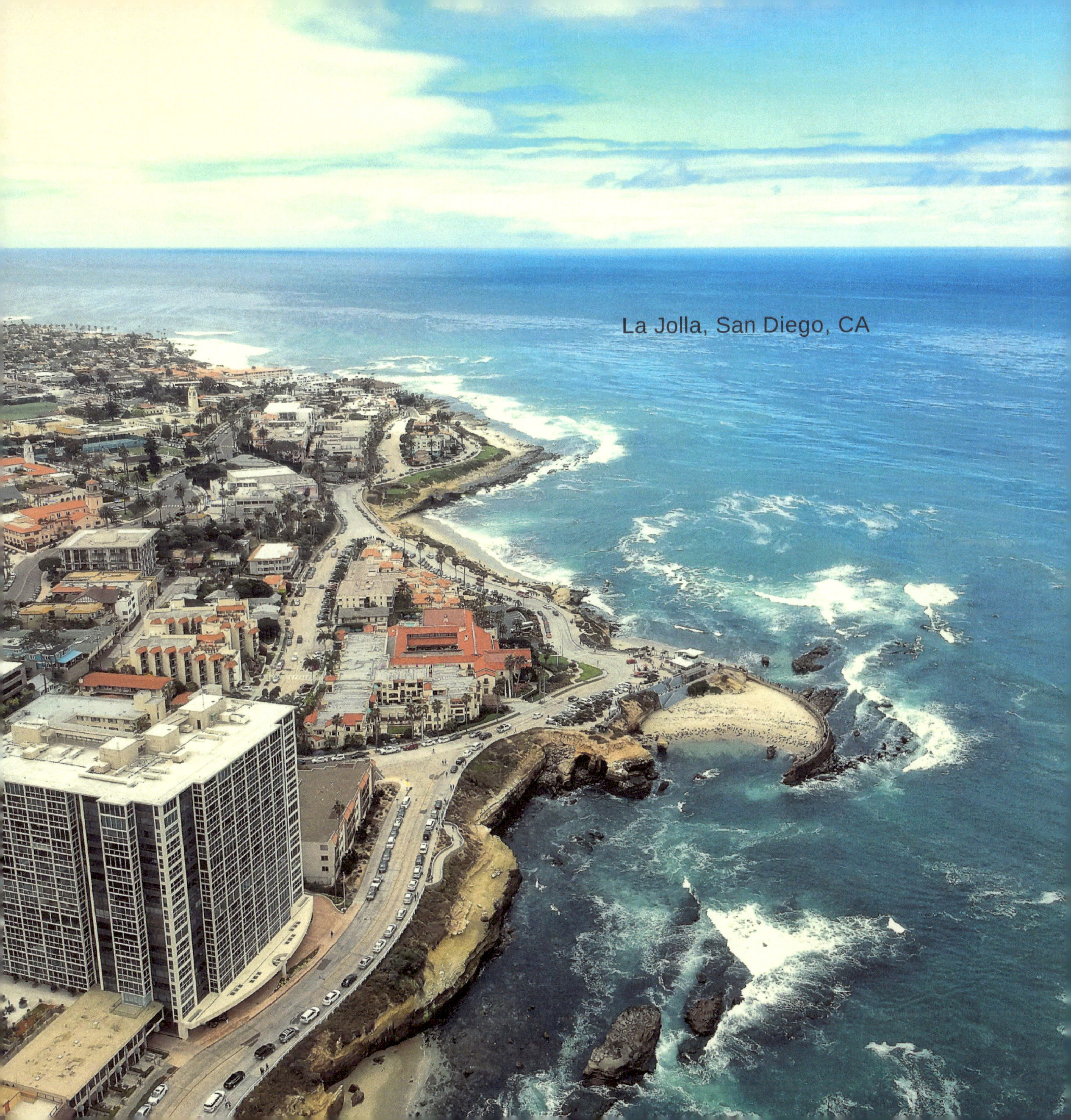
La Jolla, San Diego, CA

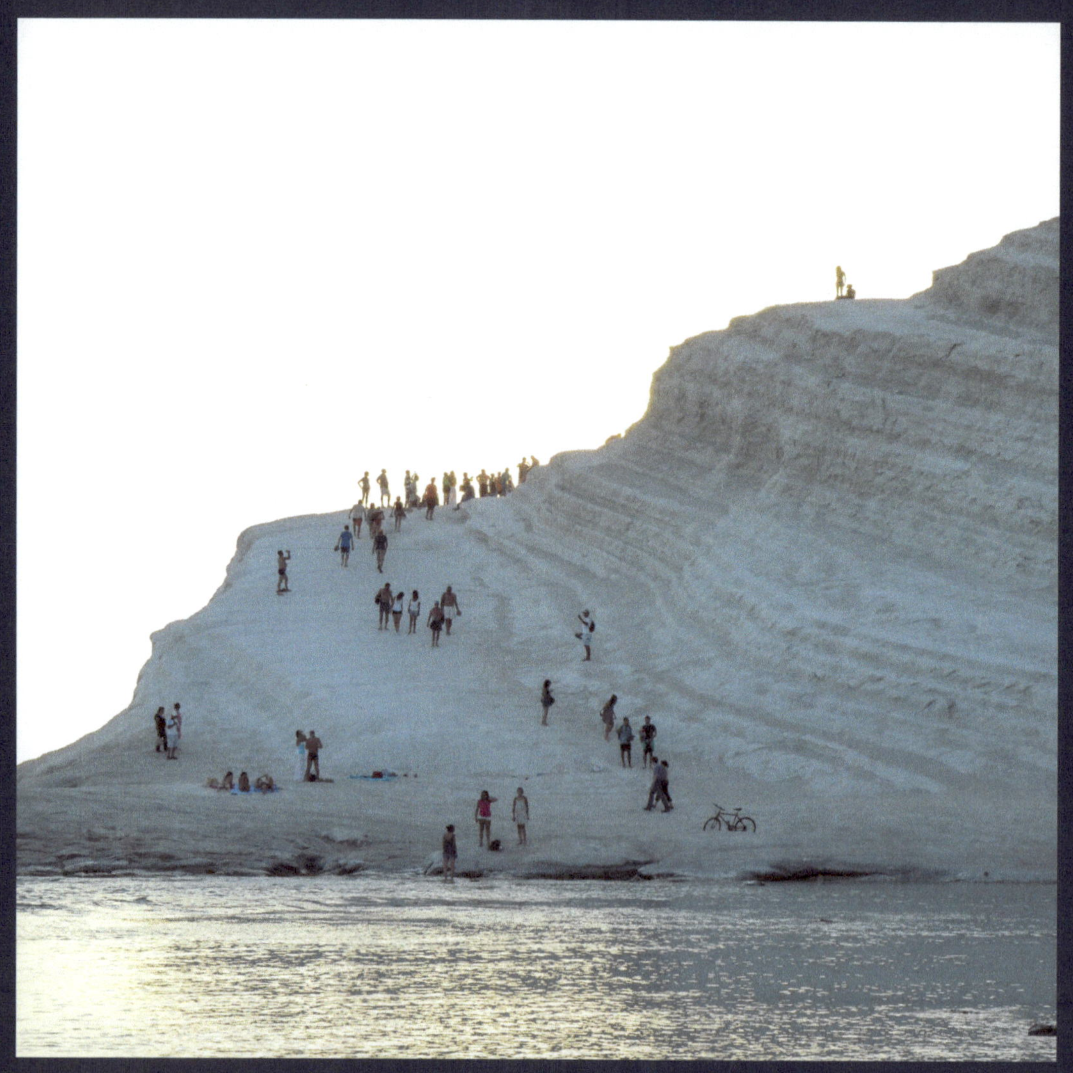

Scala dei Turchi, Sicily

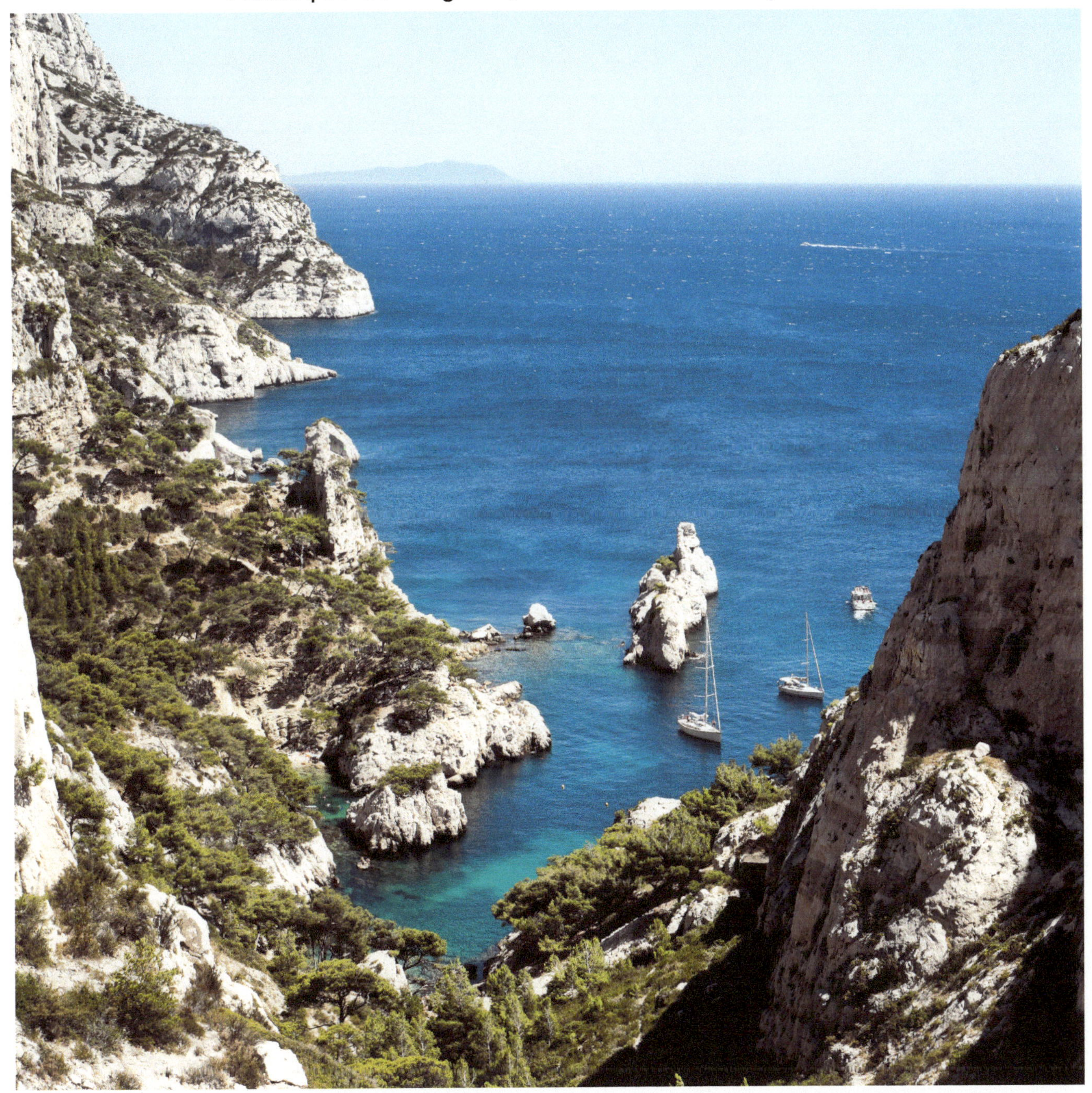

Calanque de Sugiton, Massif des Calanques

Reynisfjara Beach, Iceland

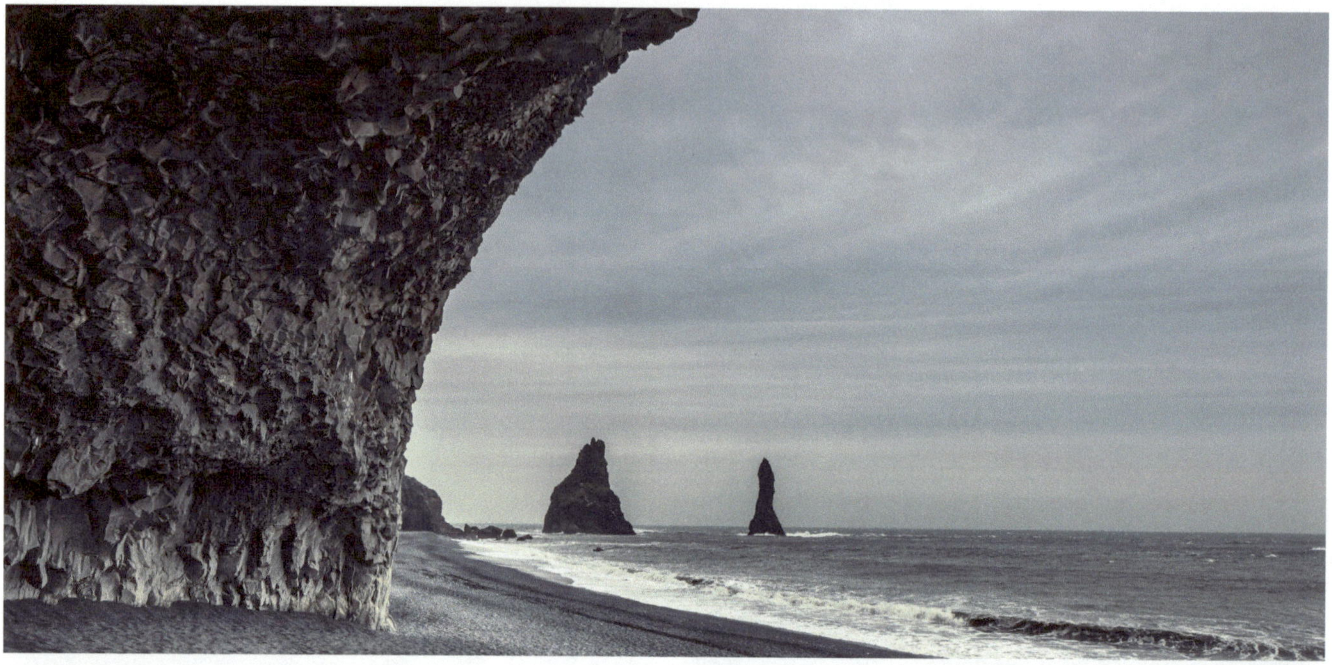

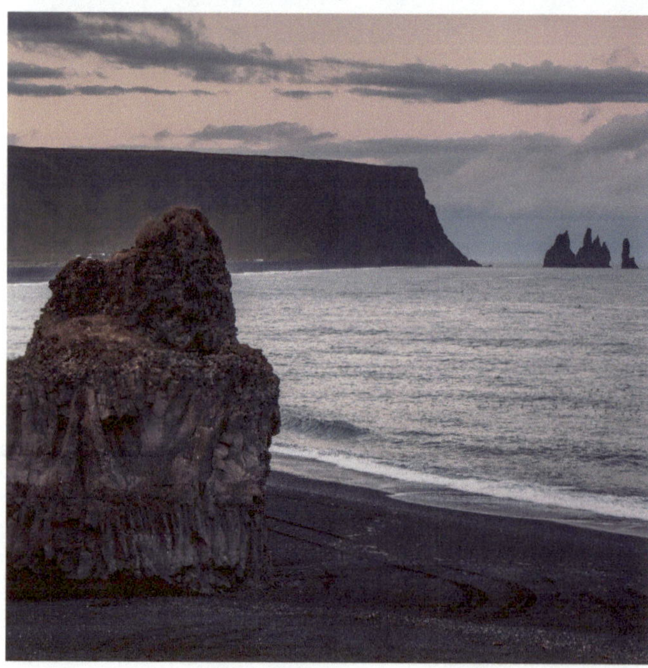

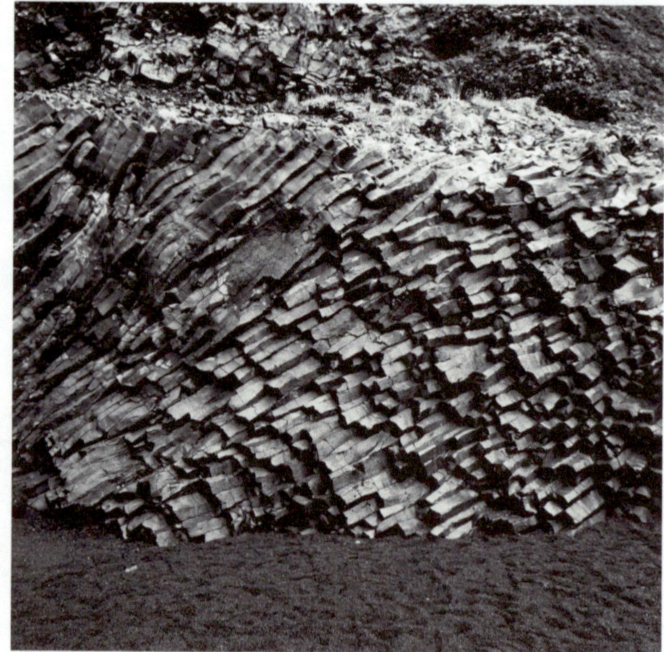

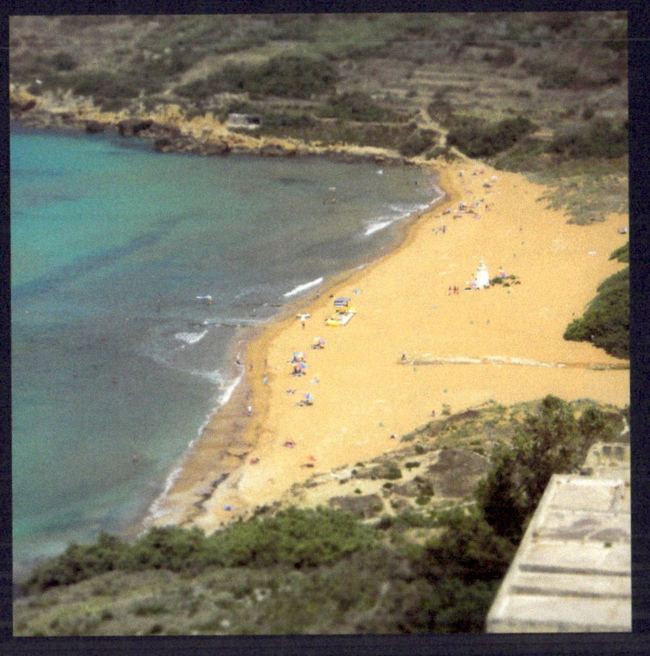

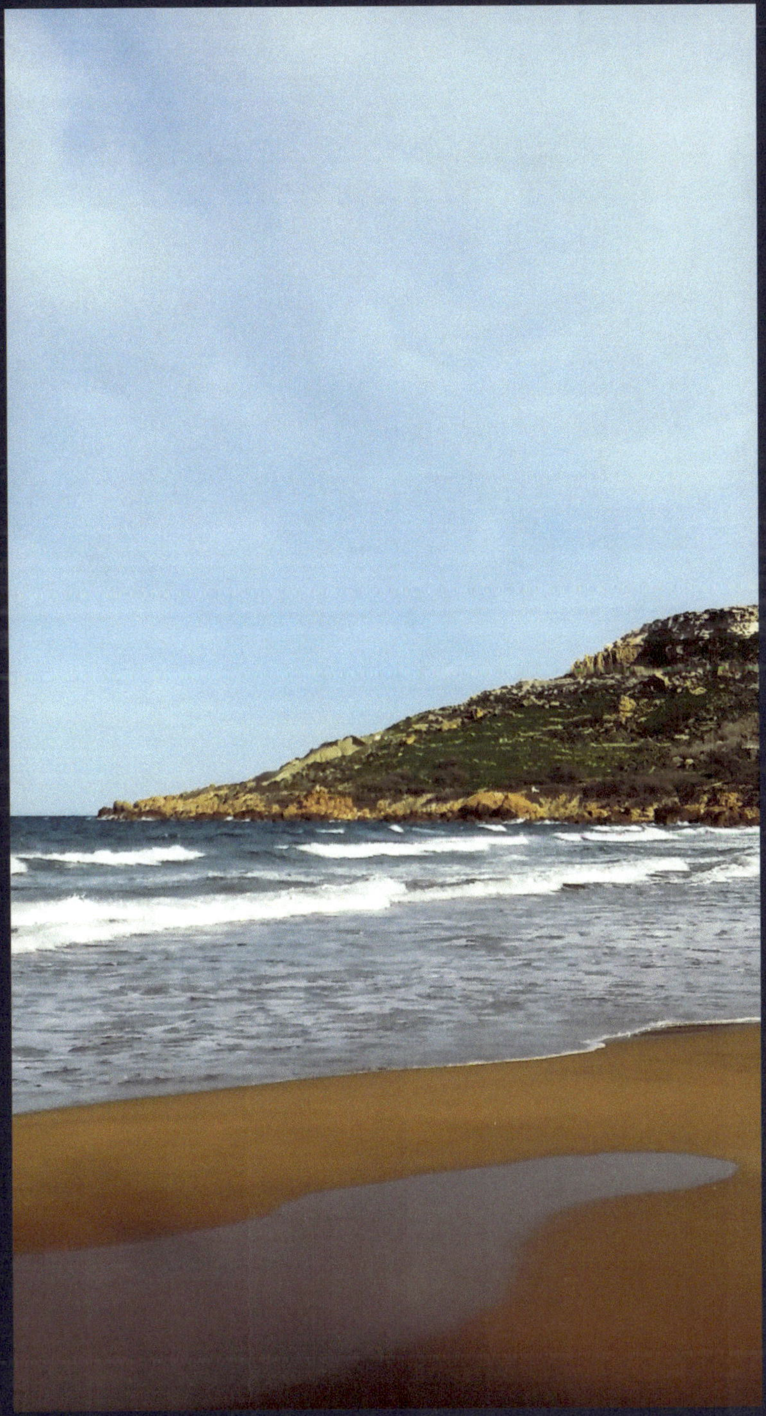

Ramla beach, Malta

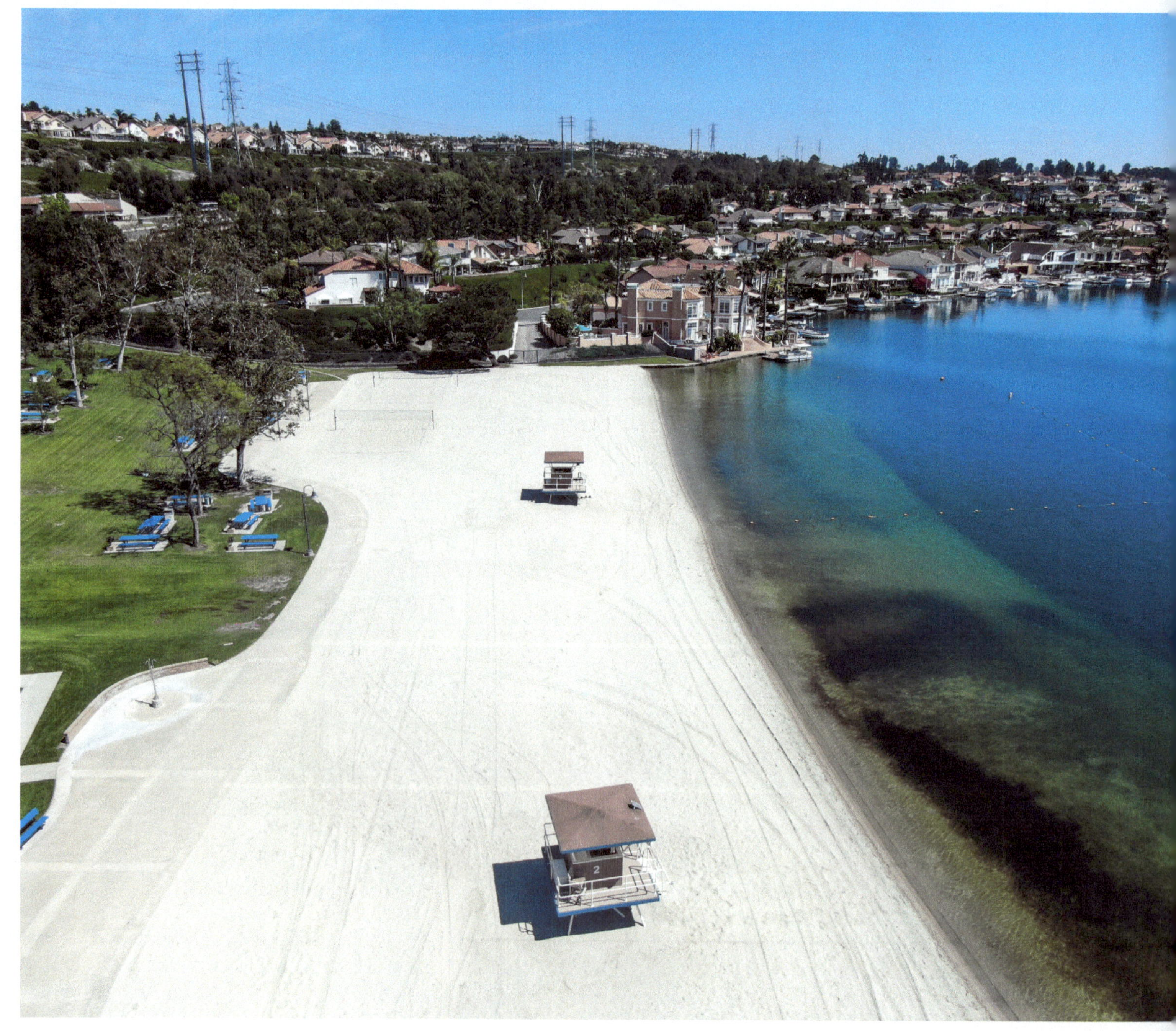

Playa Norte, Isla Mujeres

Calanque d'En-vau, France

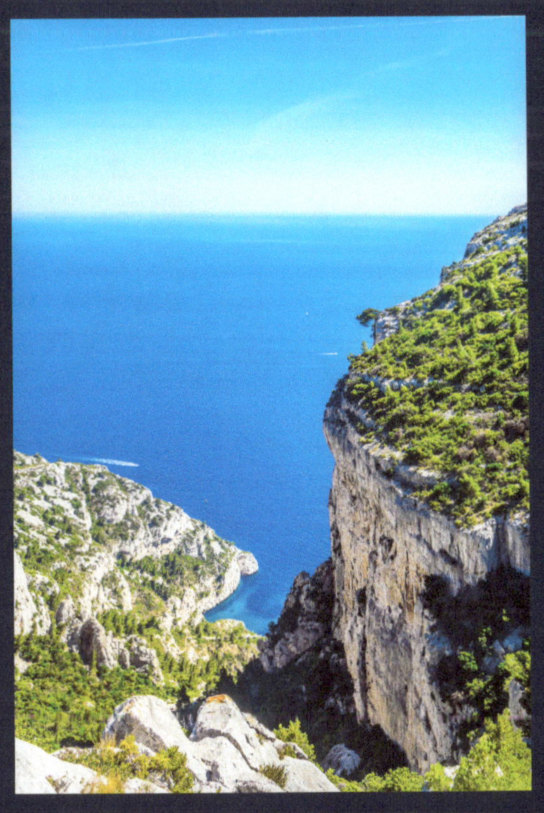

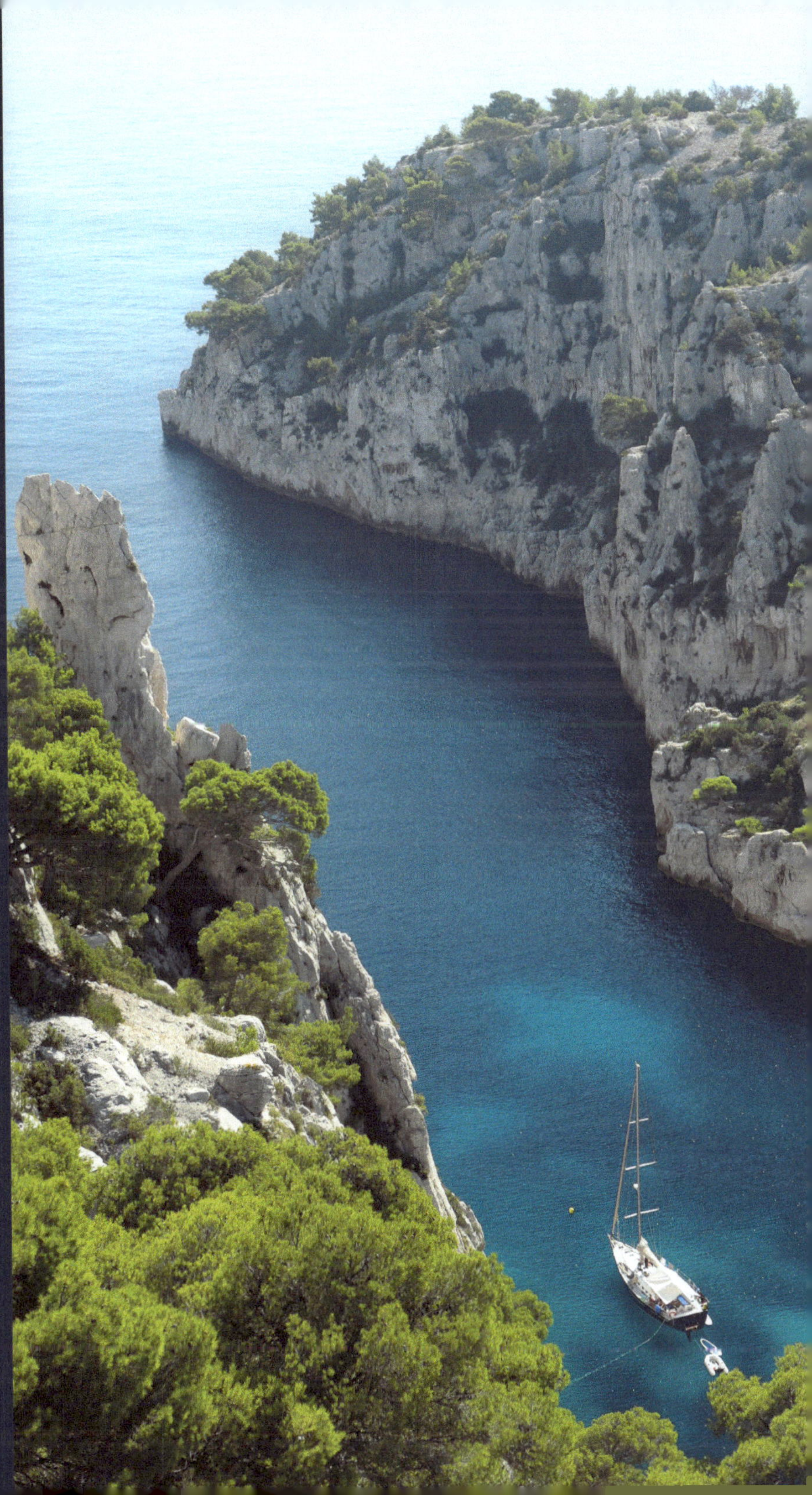

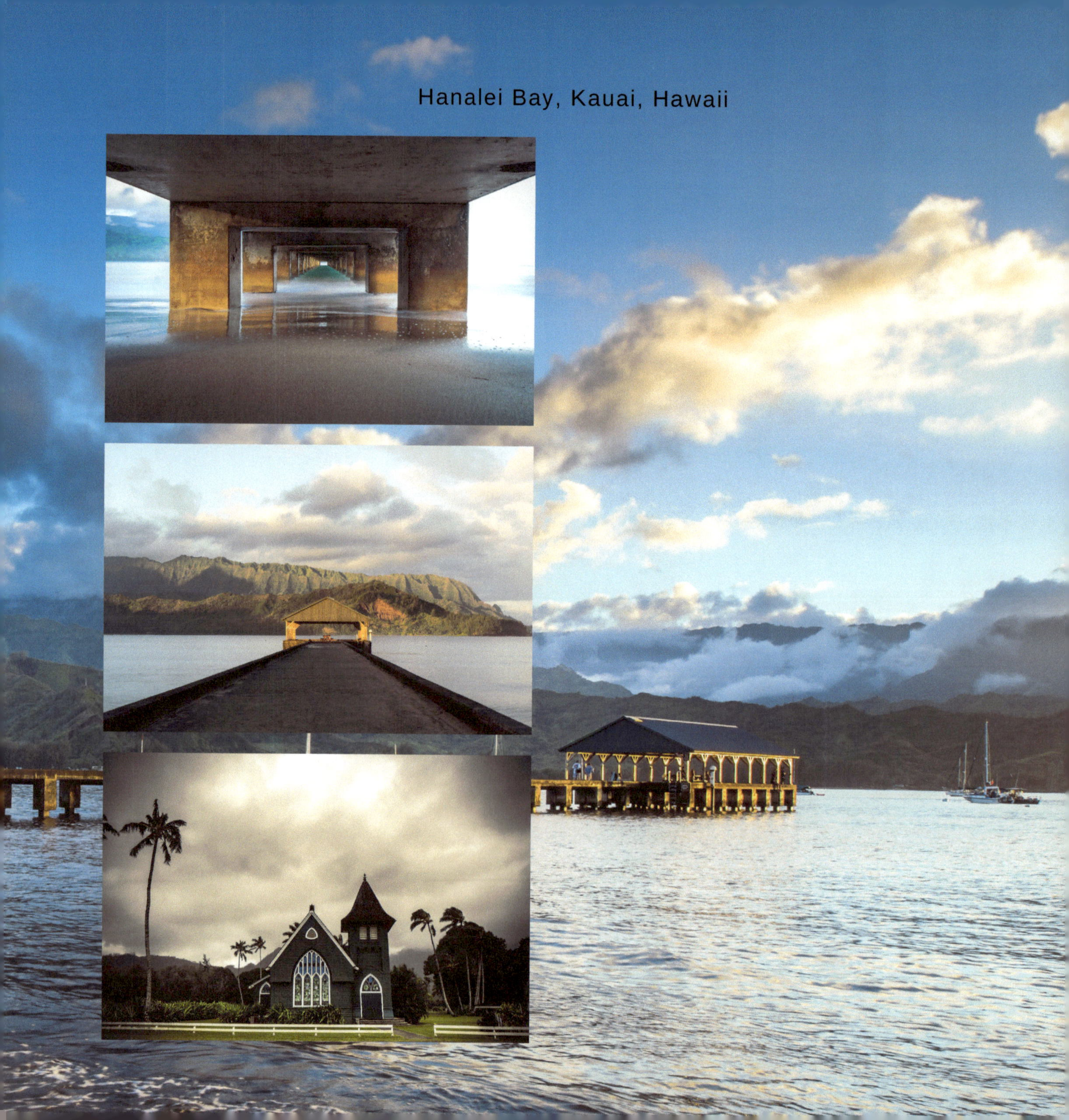

Hanalei Bay, Kauai, Hawaii

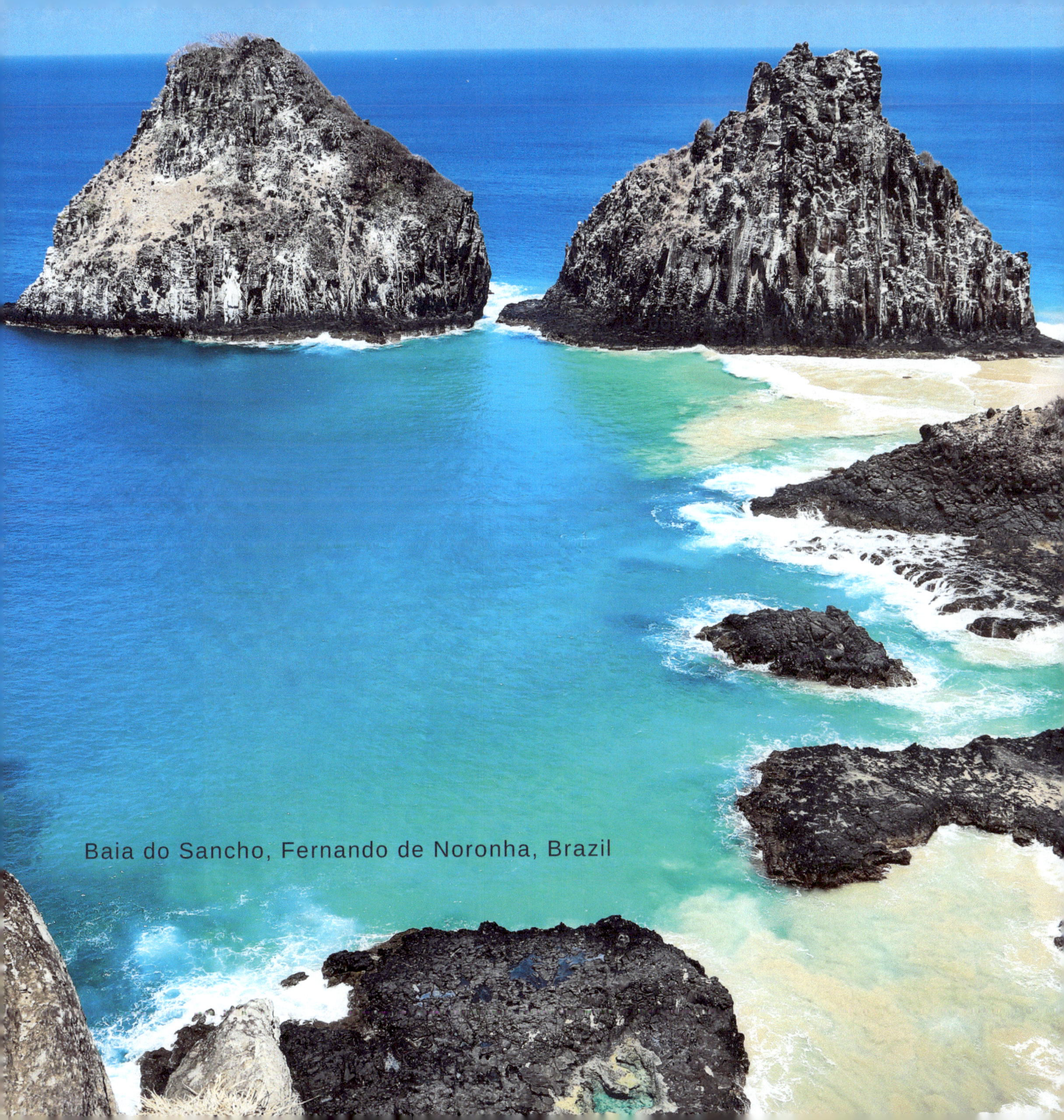

Baia do Sancho, Fernando de Noronha, Brazil

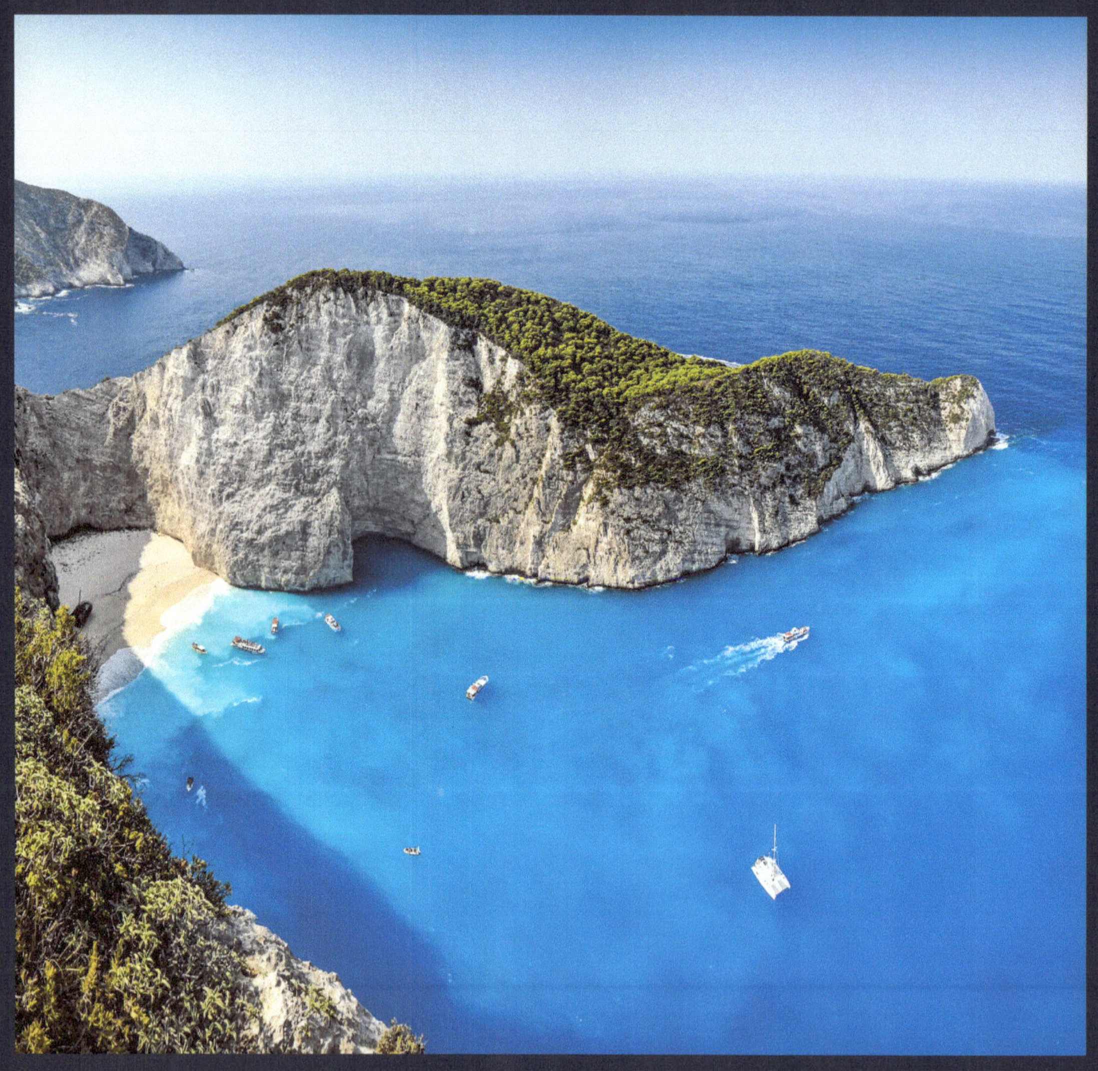

Shipwreck Beach, Zakynthos, Greece

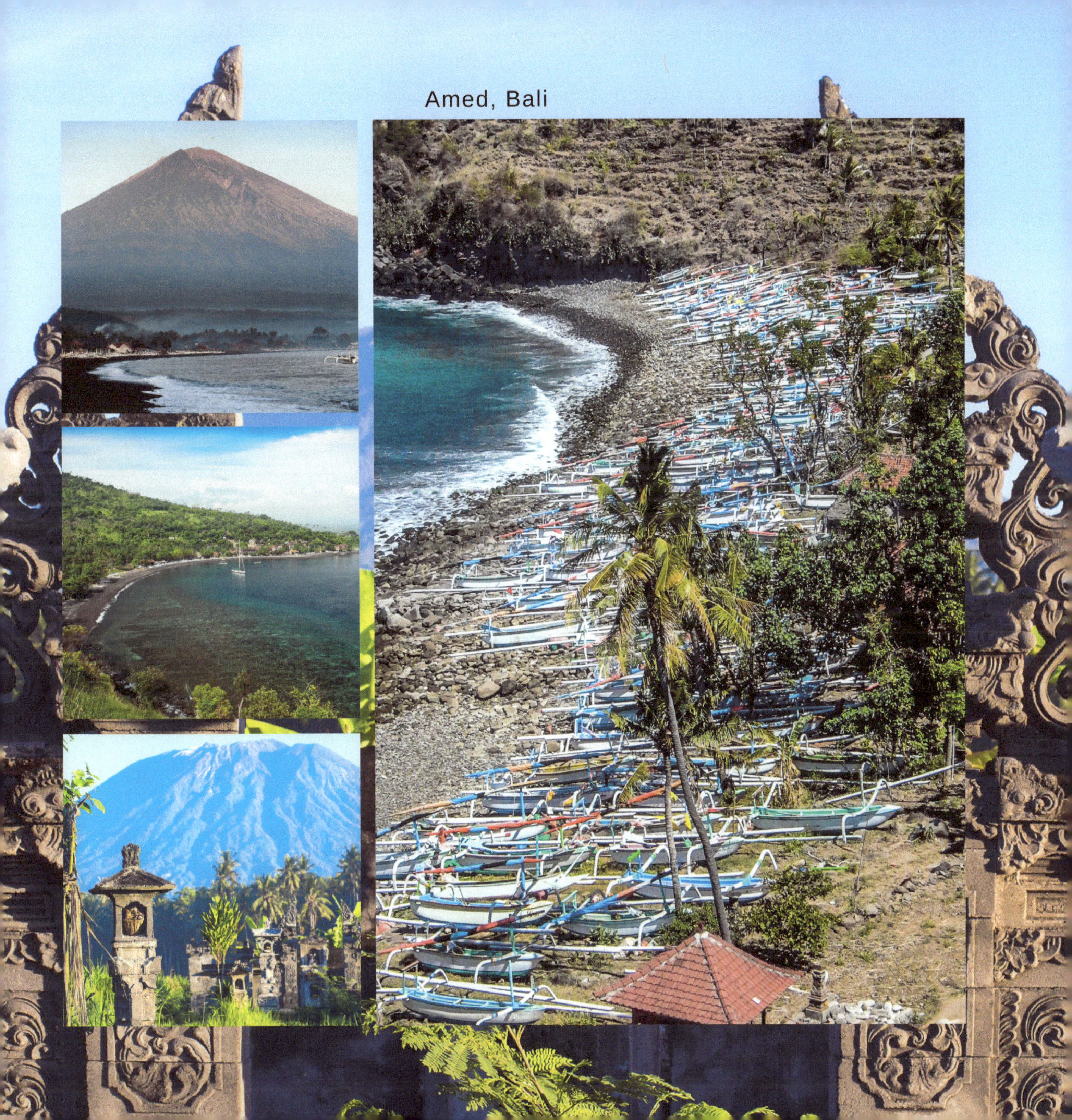
Amed, Bali

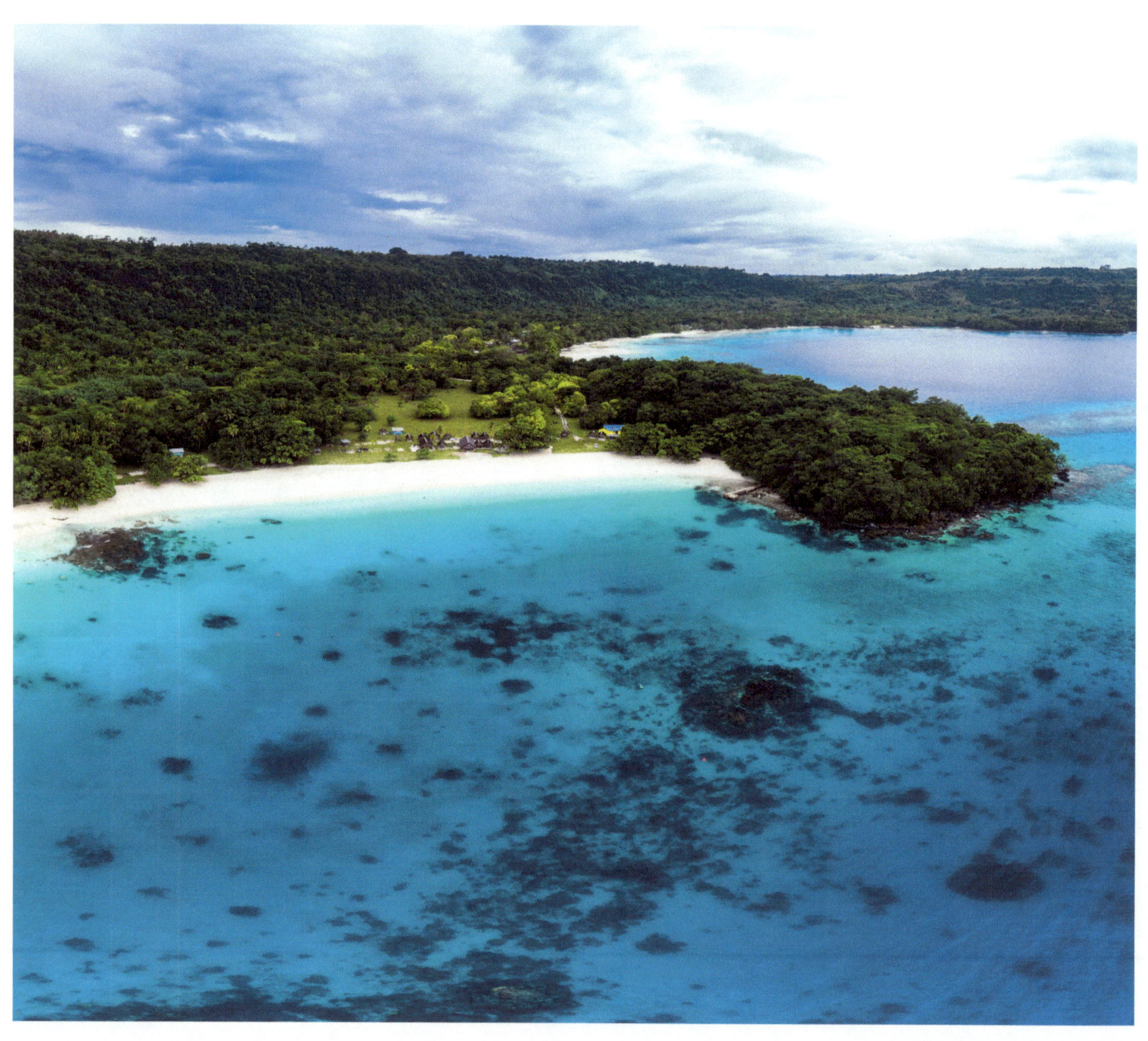

Champagne Beach (Vanuatu)

WineGlass Bay, Tasmania

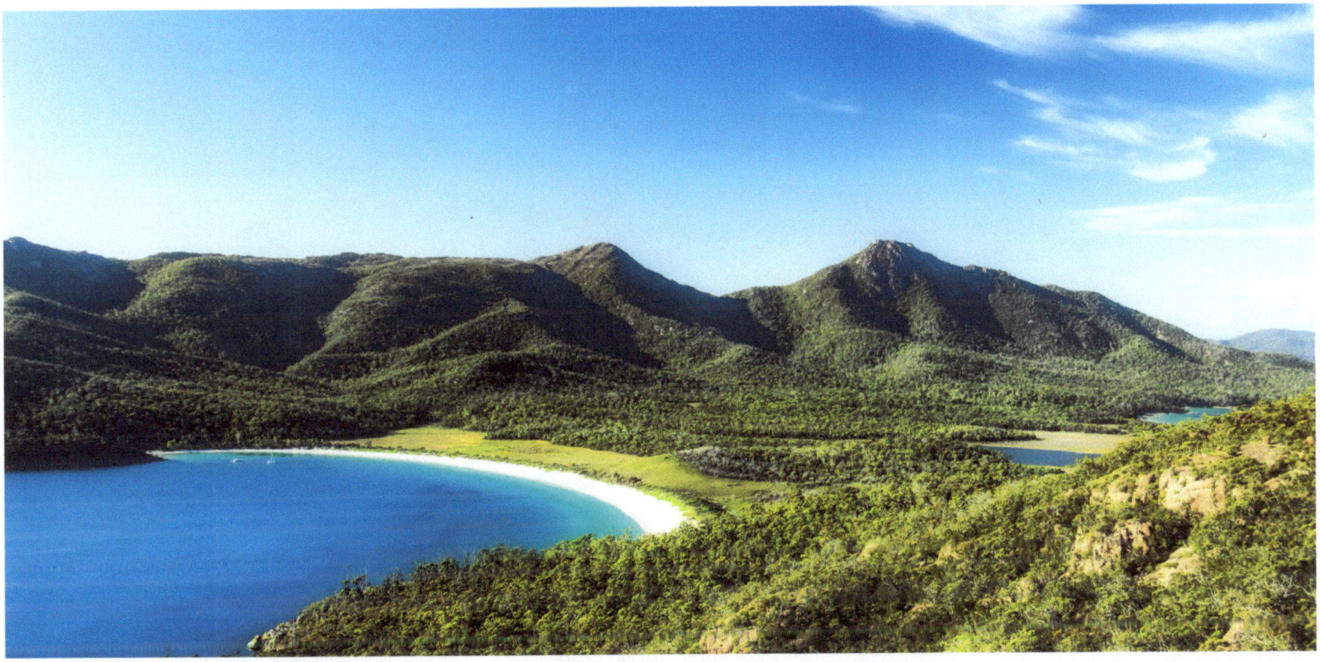

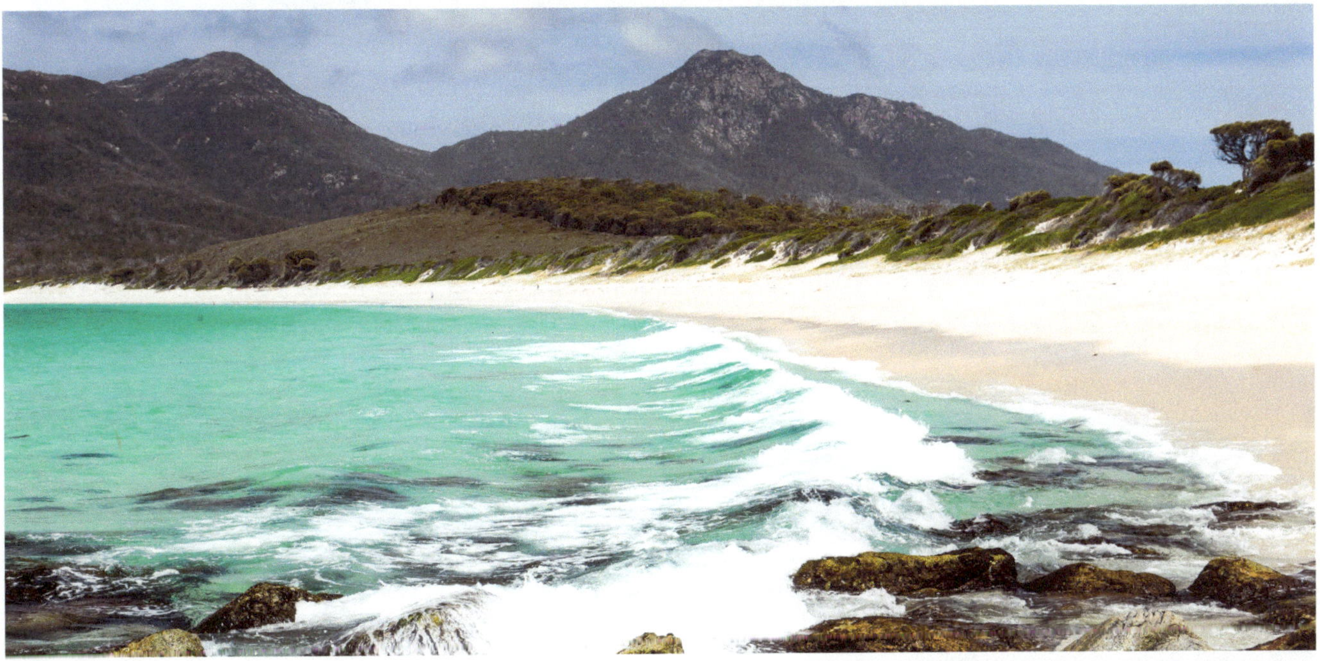

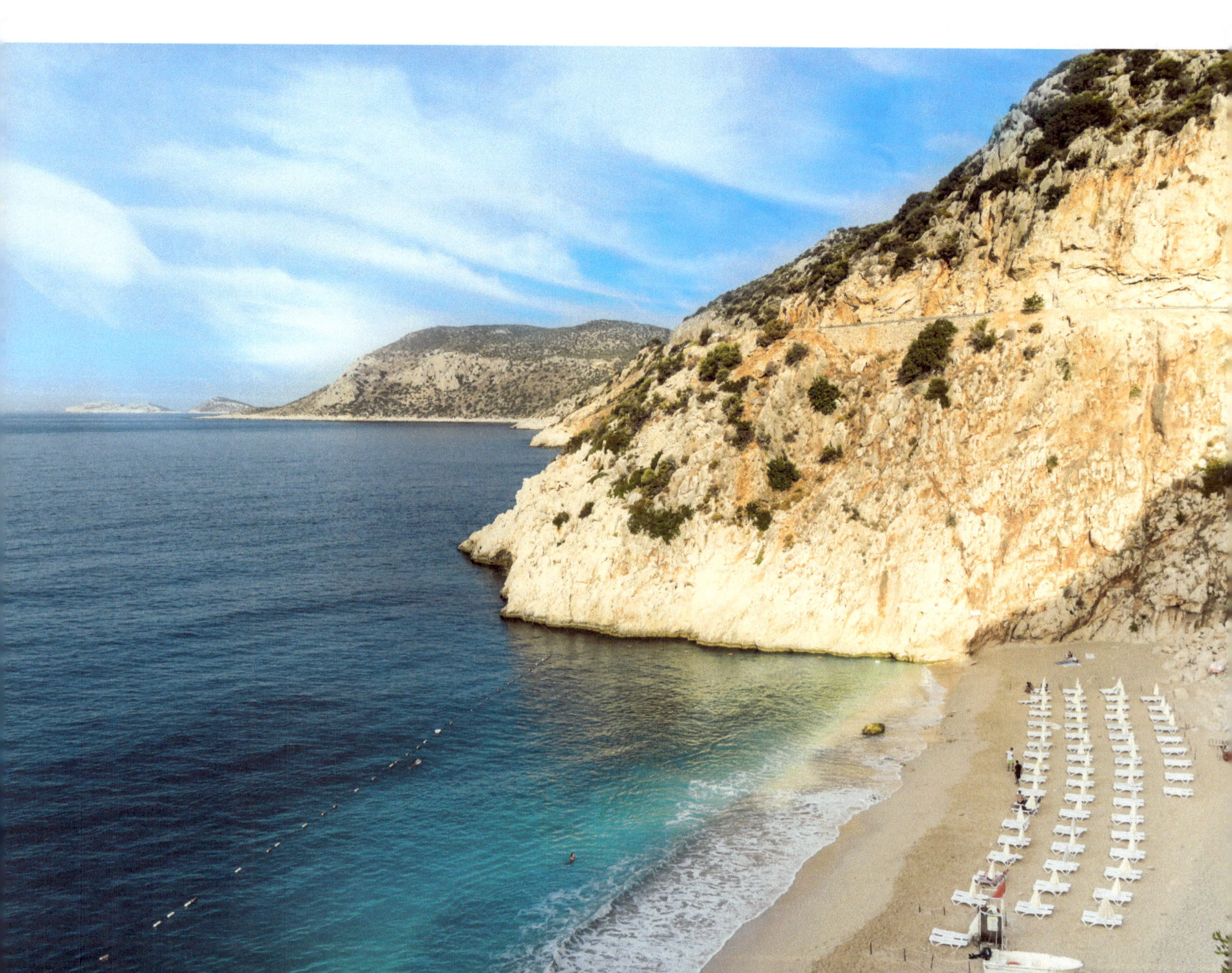

Kaputas Beach, Turkey

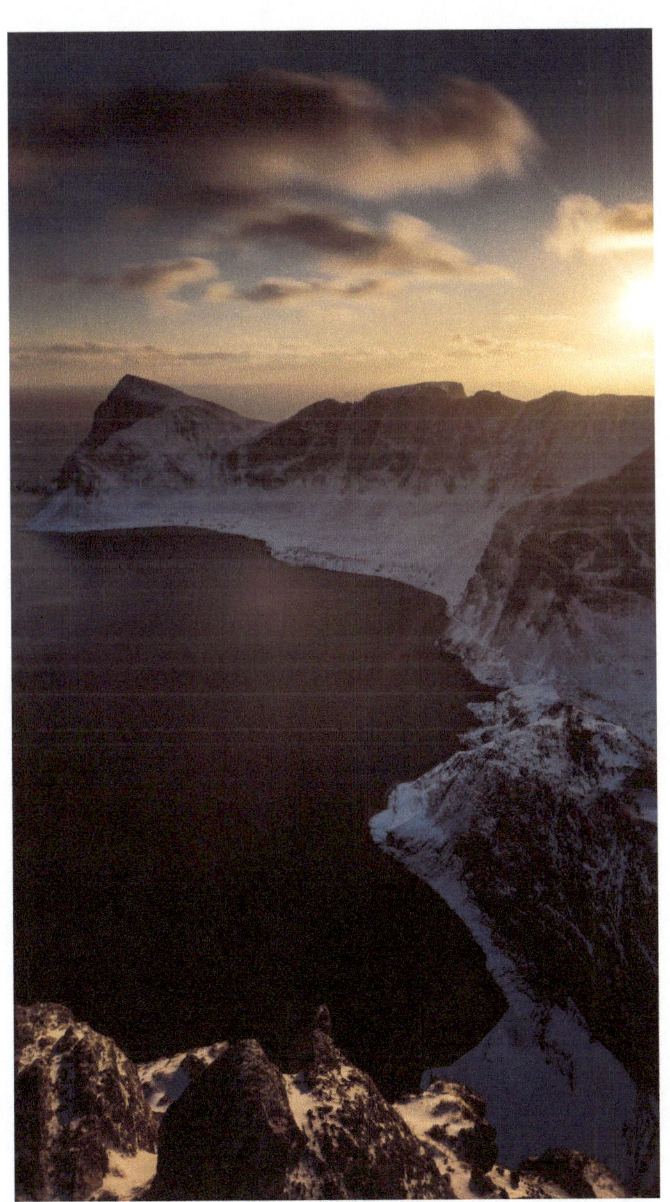

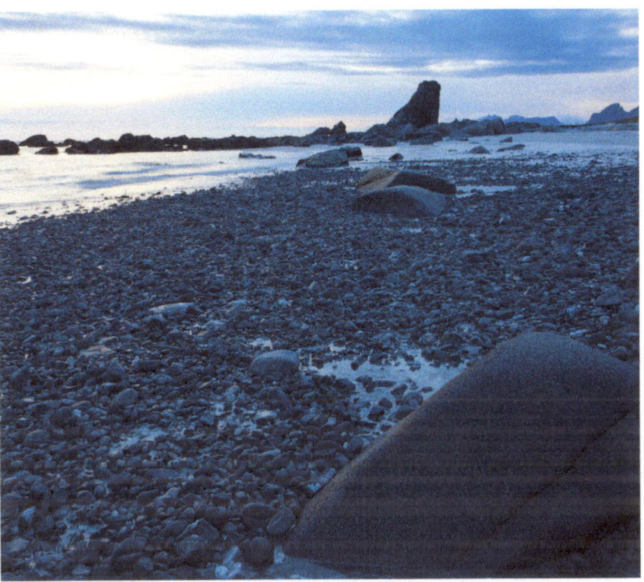

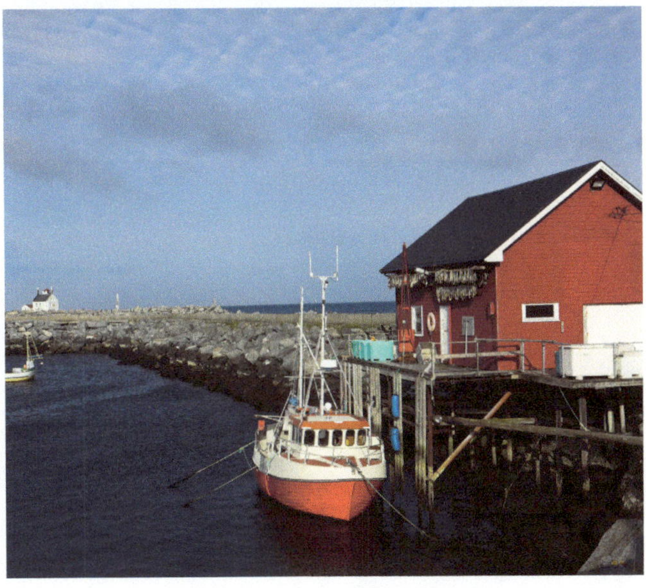

Vaeroy Beach, Norway

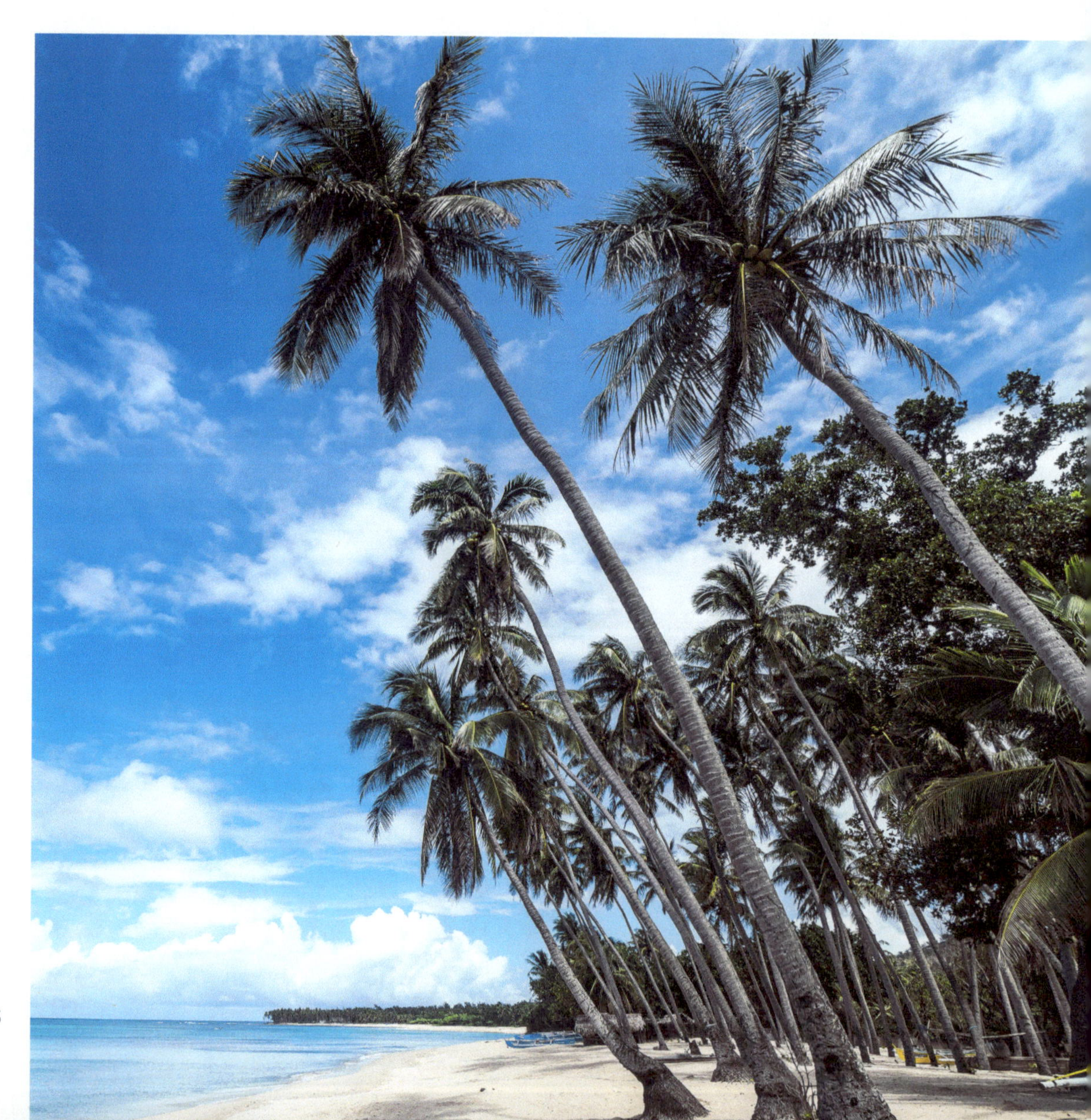

Saud Beach,
Luzon, Philippines

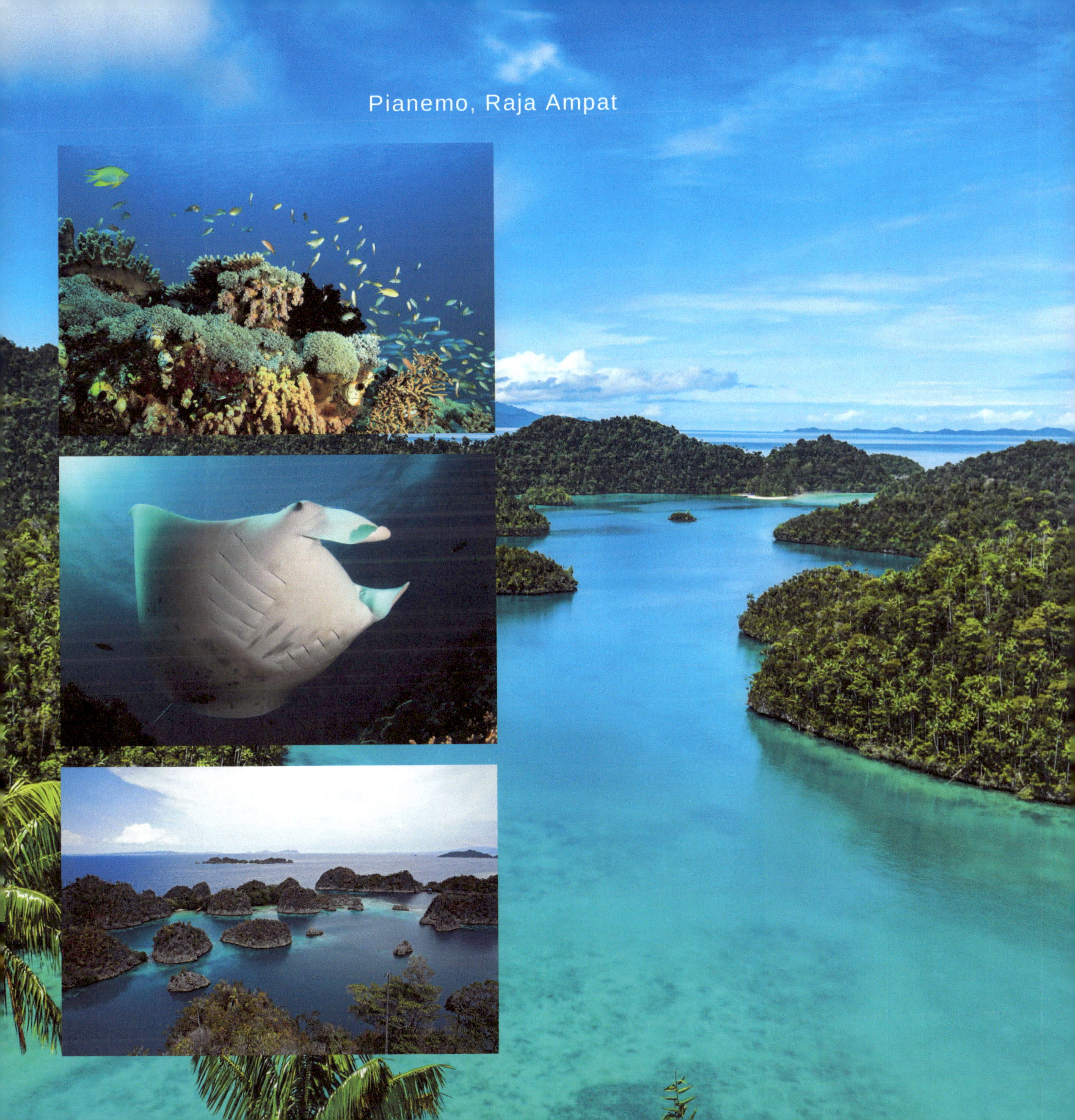

Pianemo, Raja Ampat

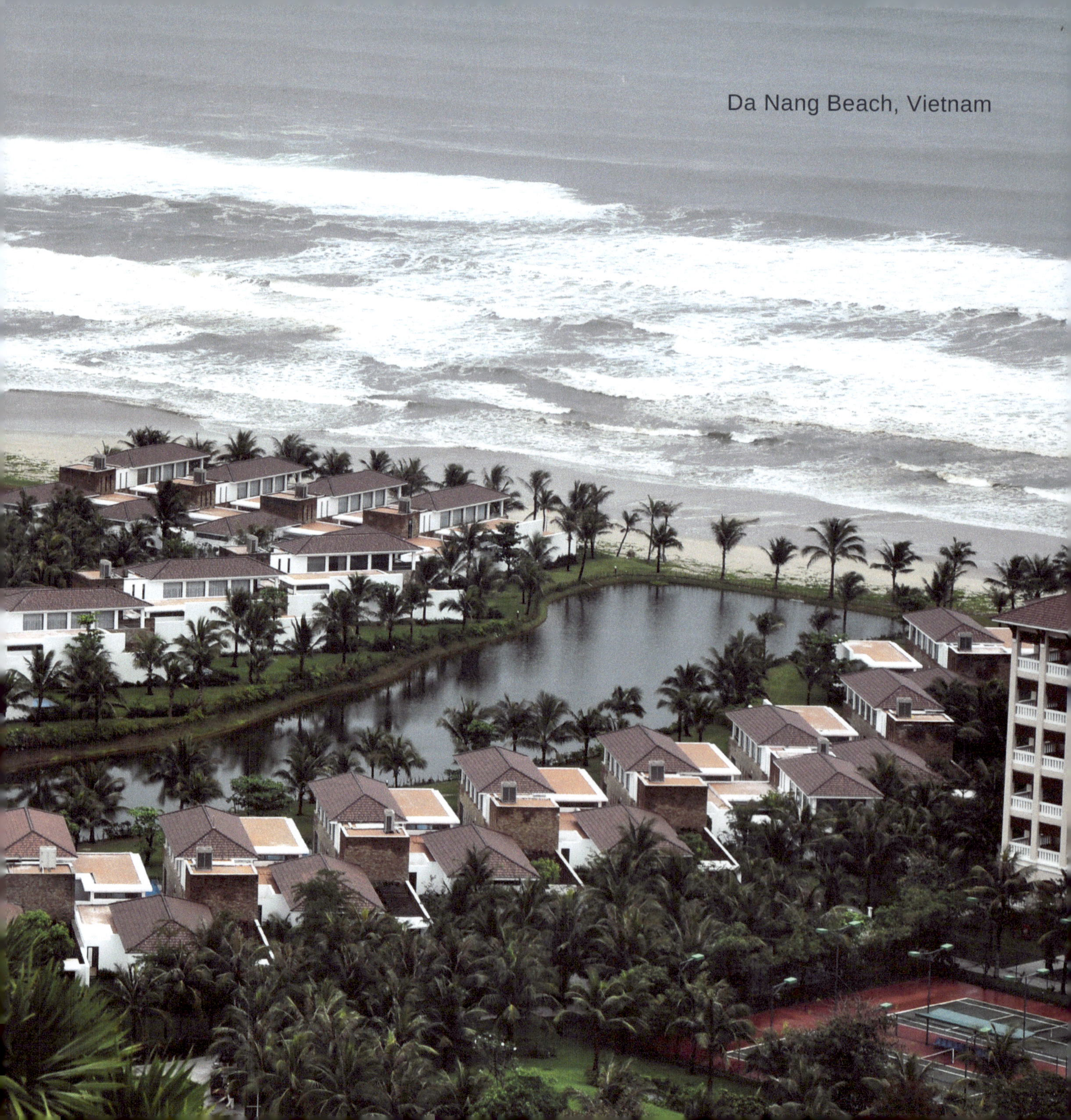
Da Nang Beach, Vietnam

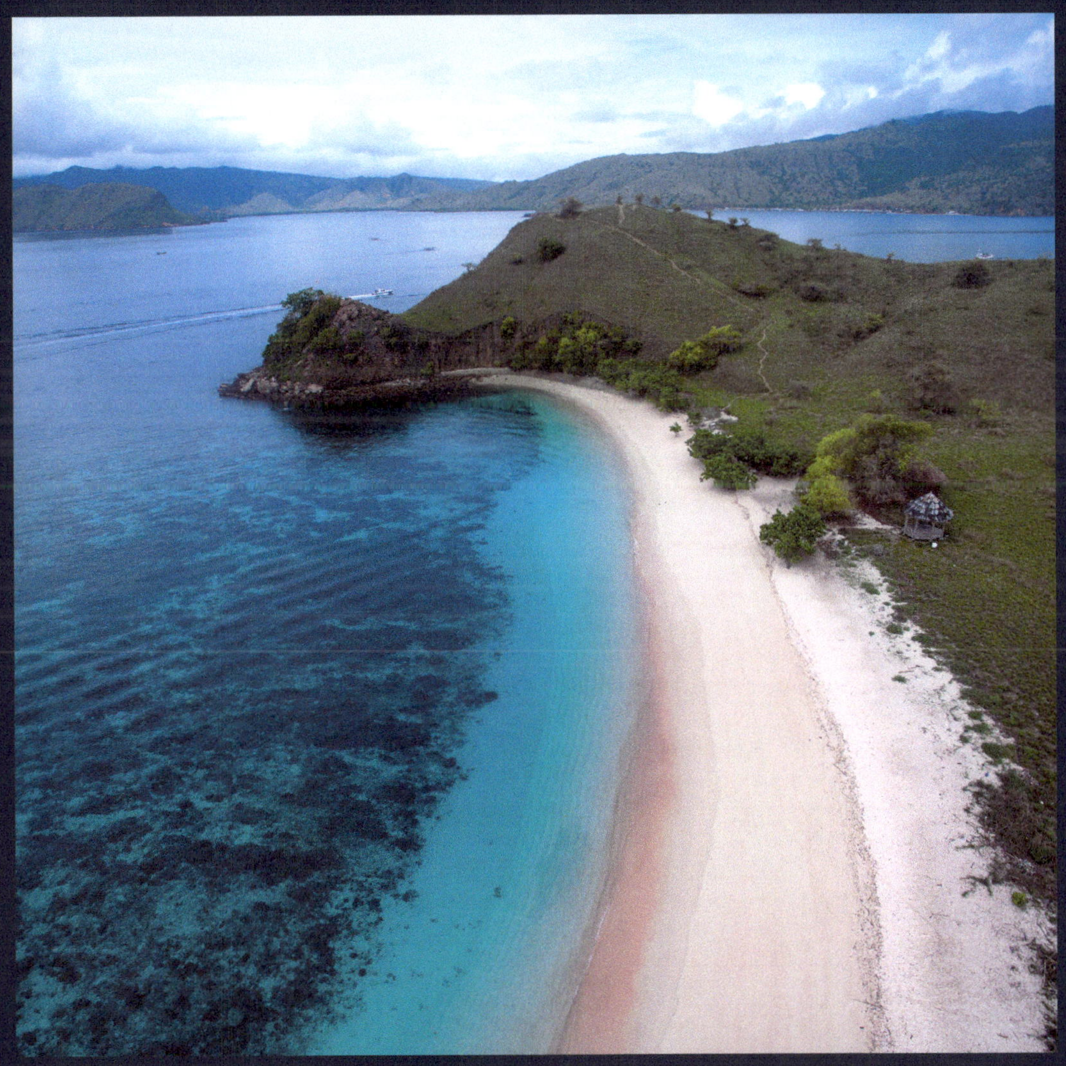

Pink Sands Beach, Harbour Island, The Bahamas

Lanikai Beach, Hawaii

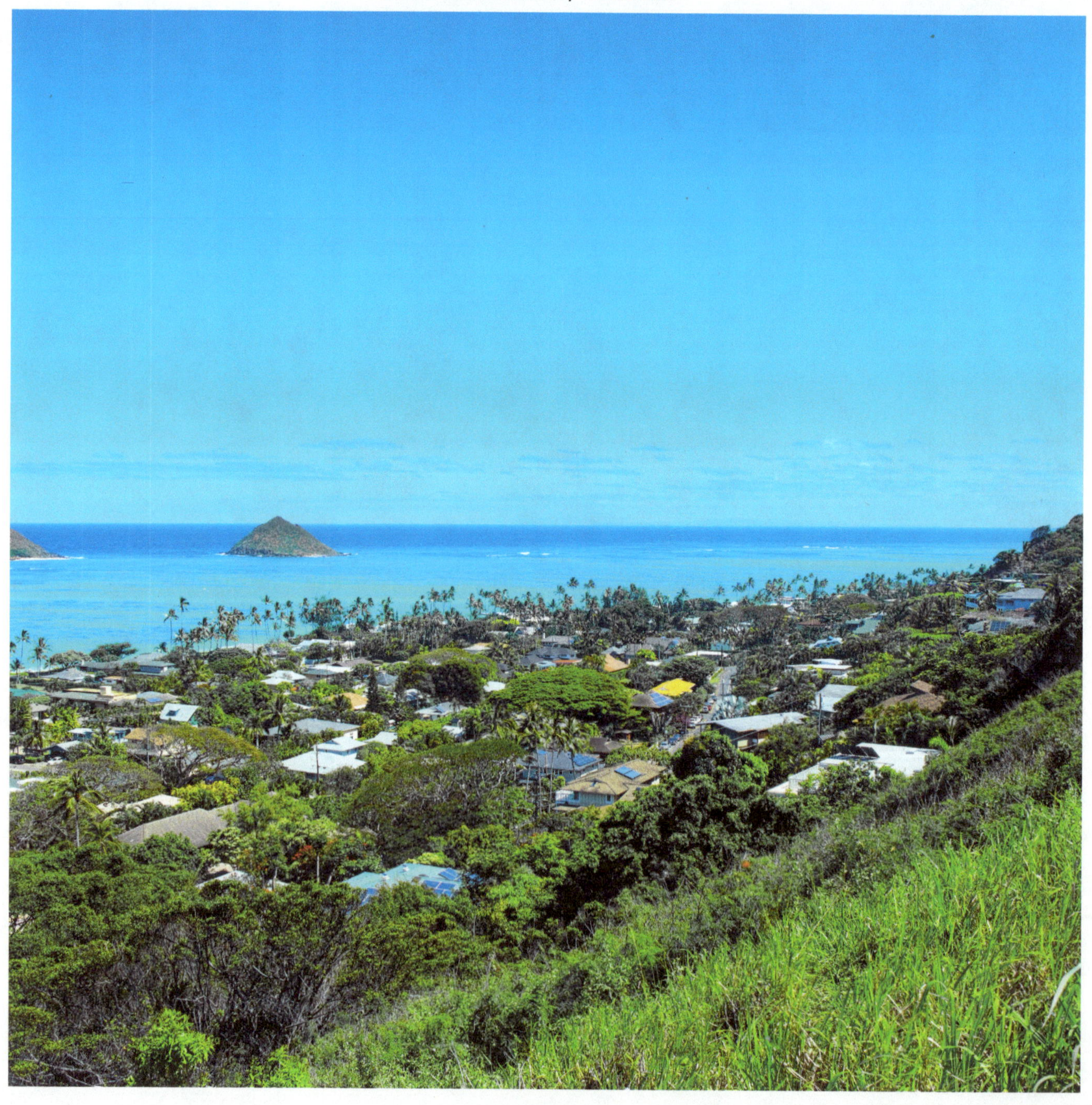

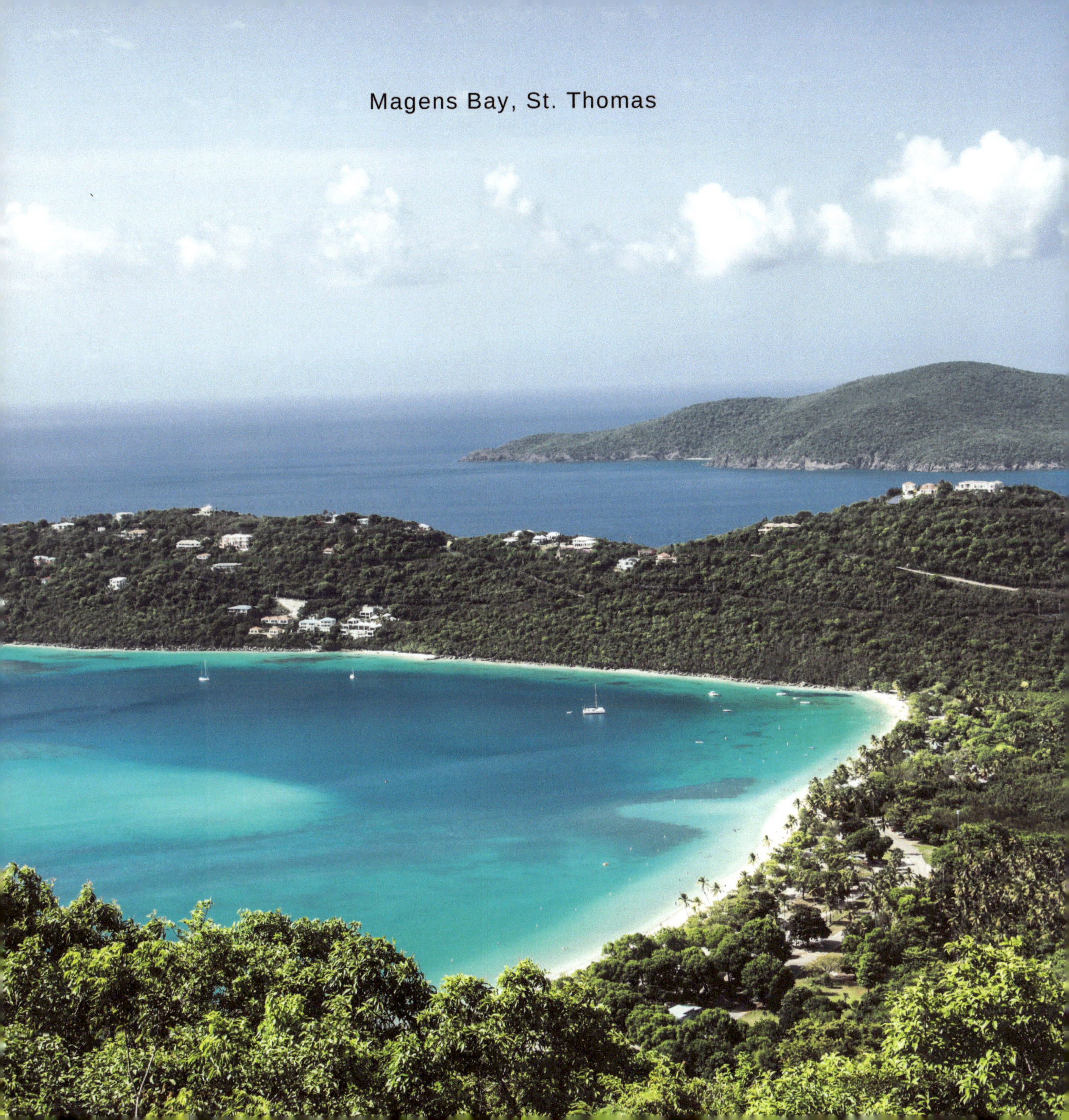

Magens Bay, St. Thomas

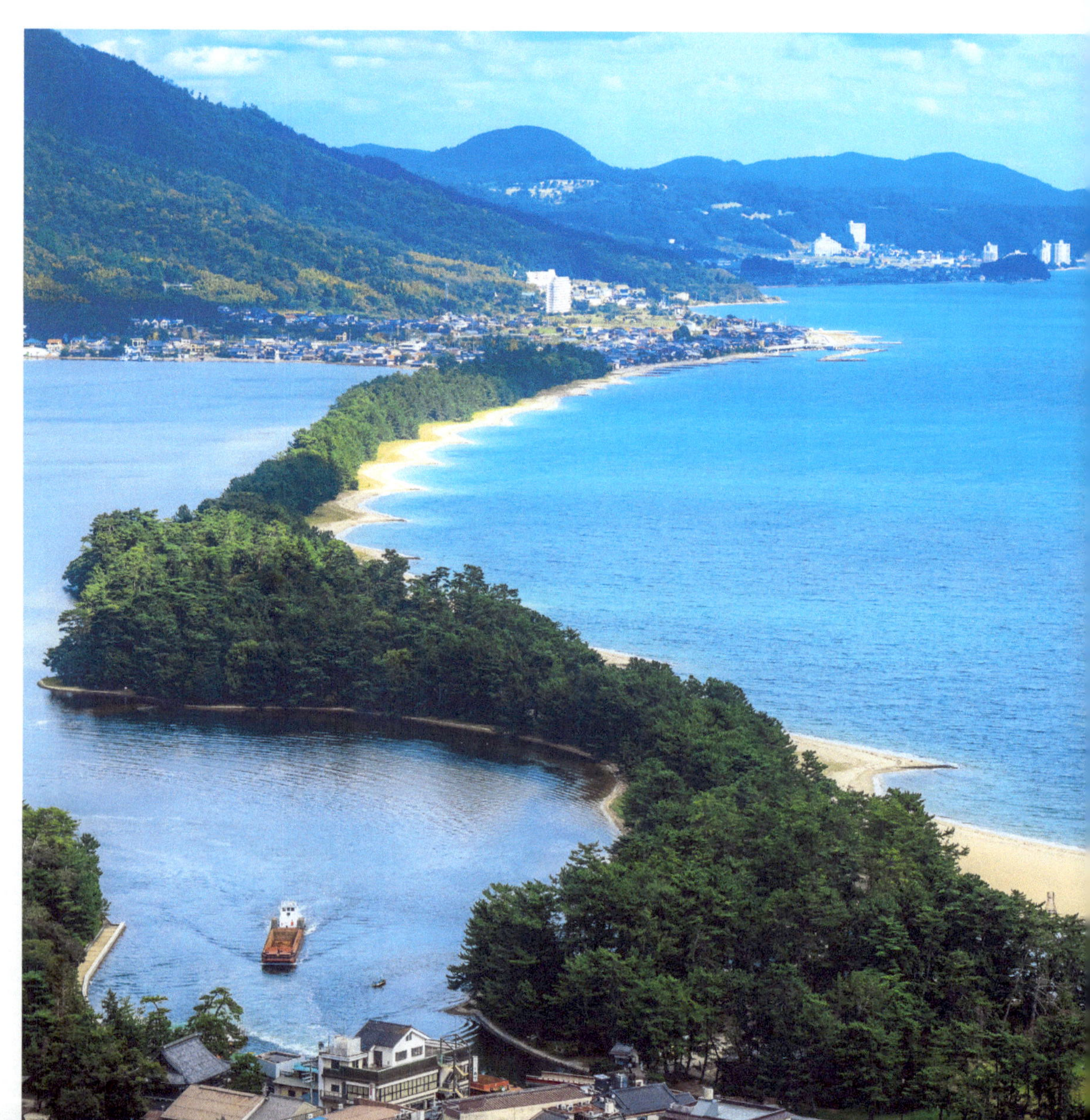

Amanohashidate,
Kyoto, Japan

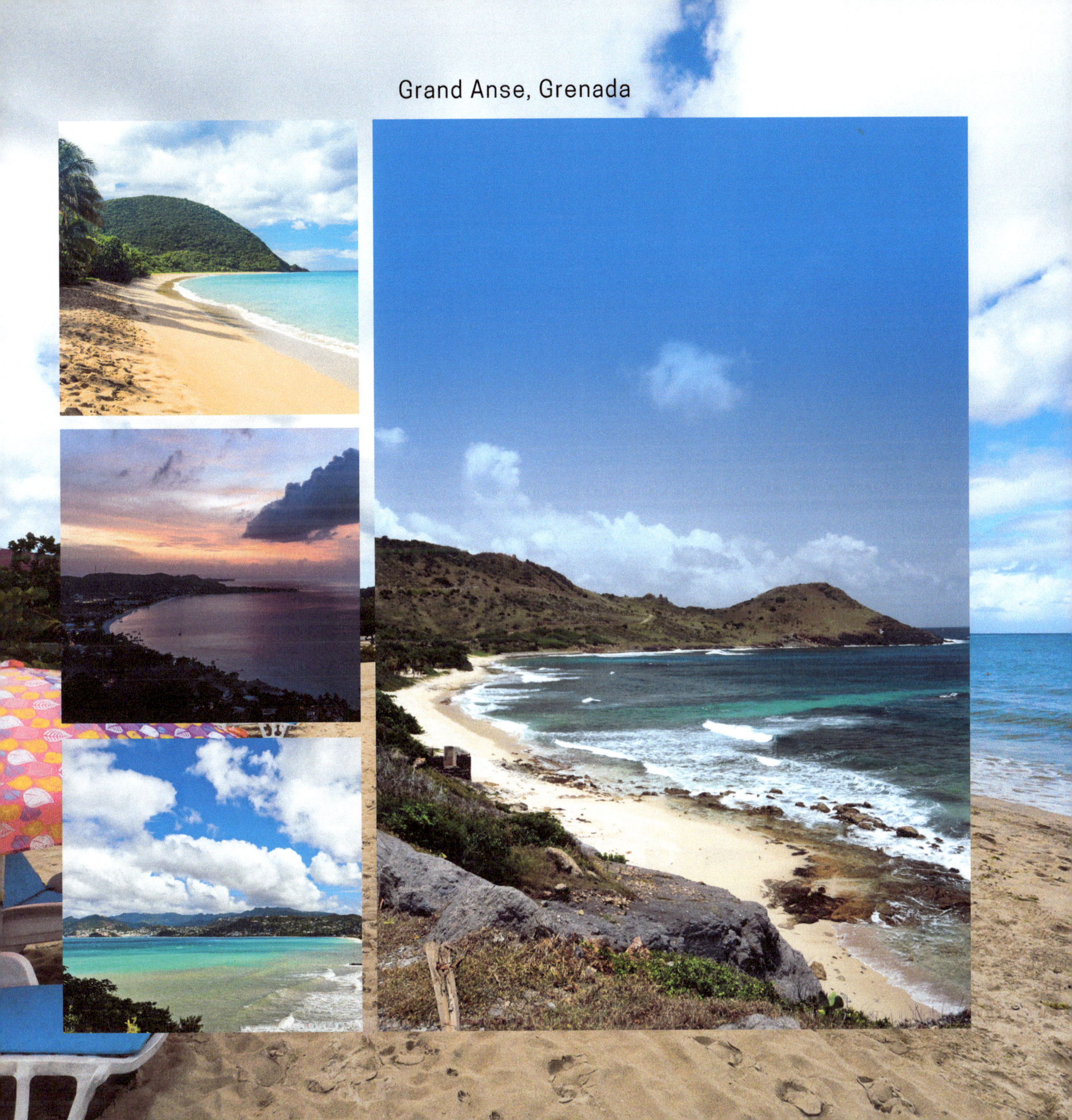

Grand Anse, Grenada

Balandra Beach, Baja California Sur

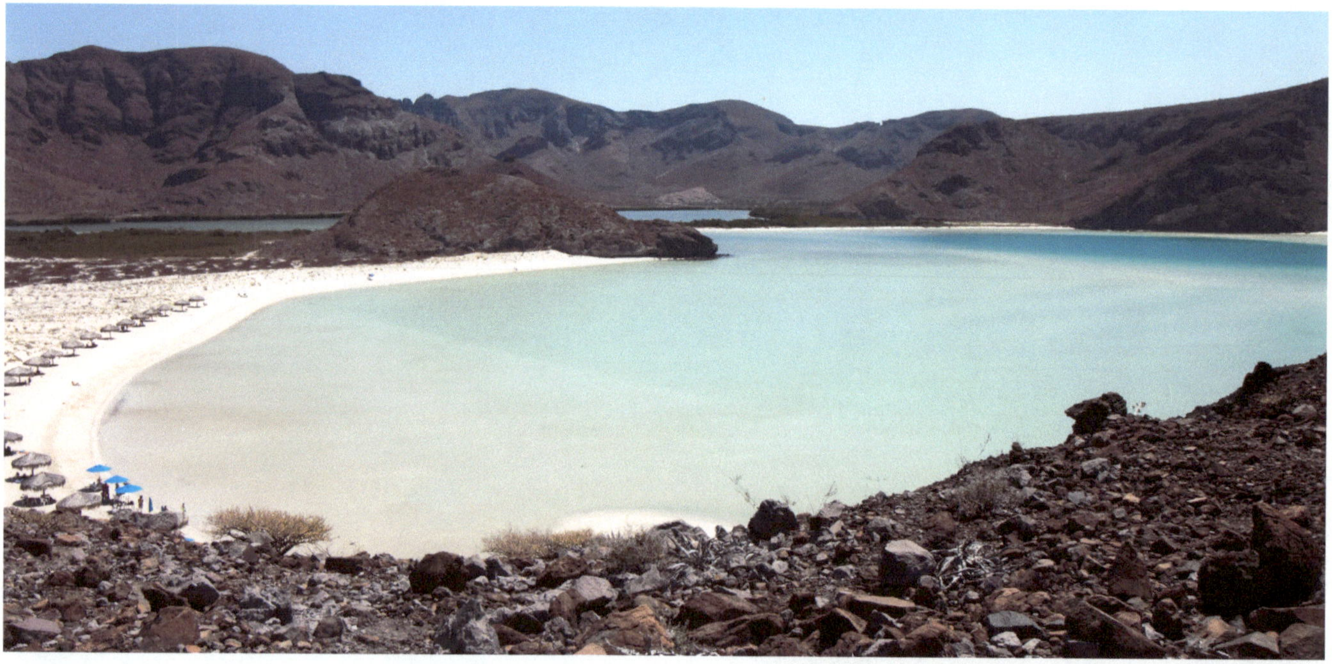

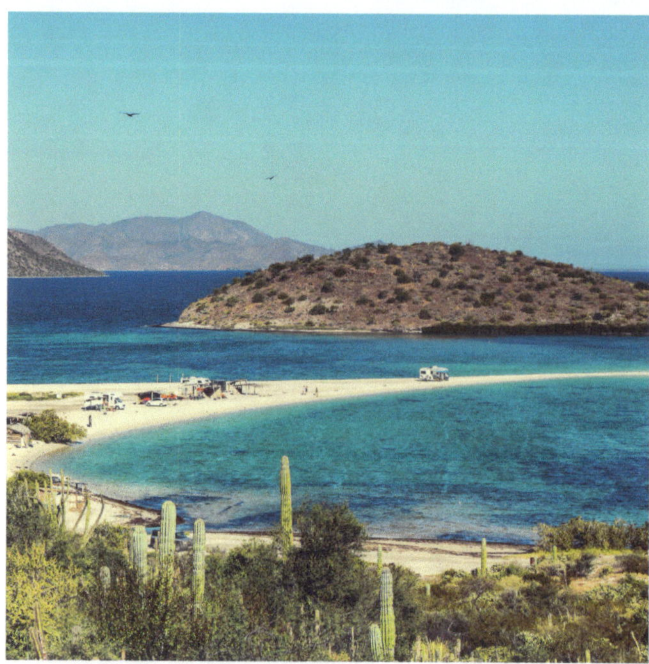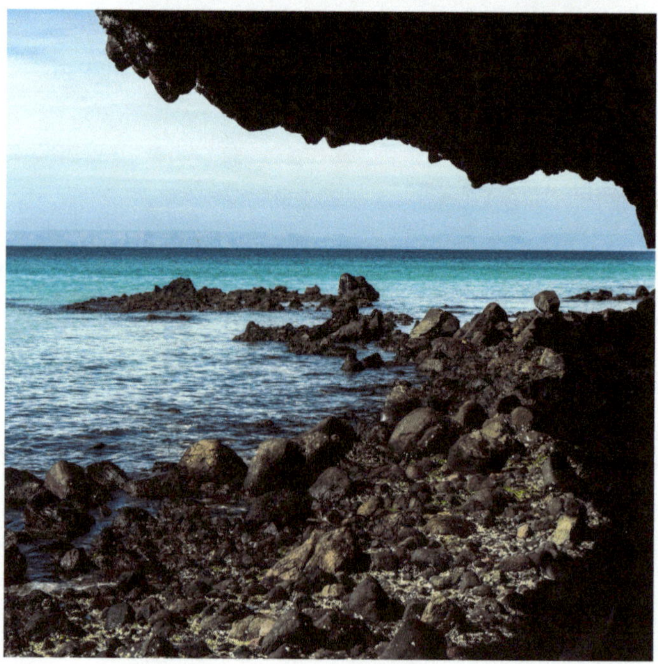

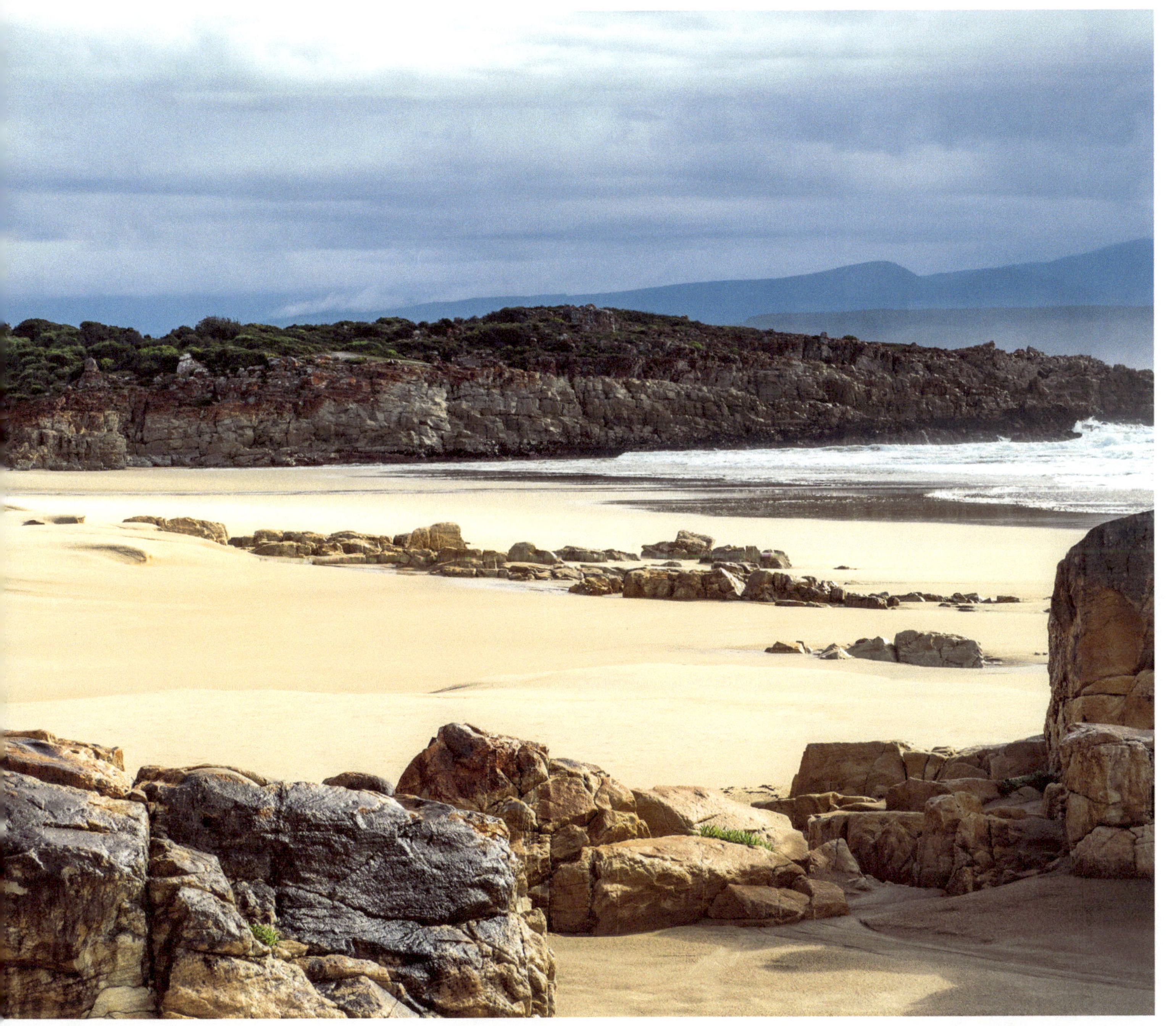

Noetzie Beach, Plettenberg Bay

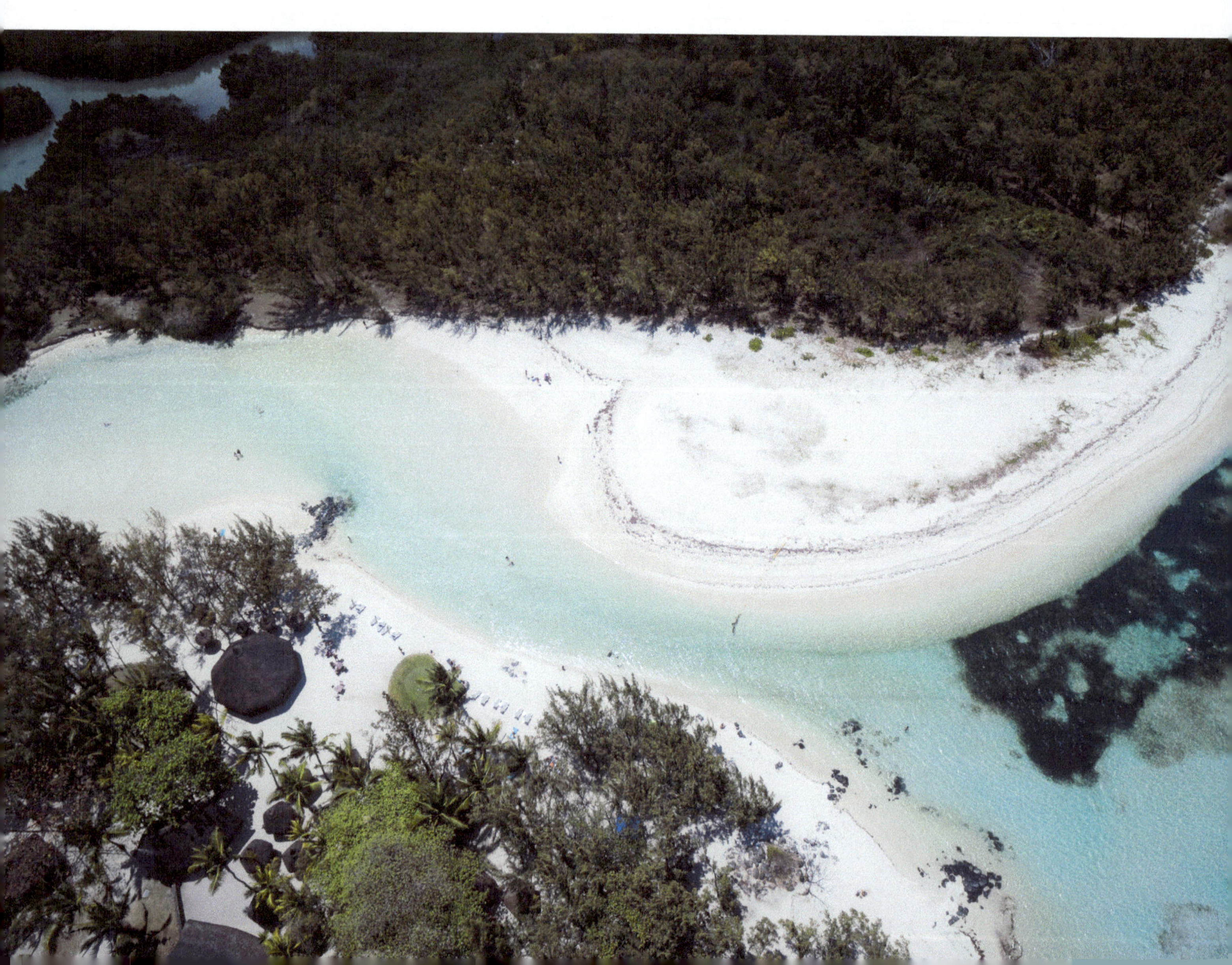

Île aux Cerfs, Mauritius

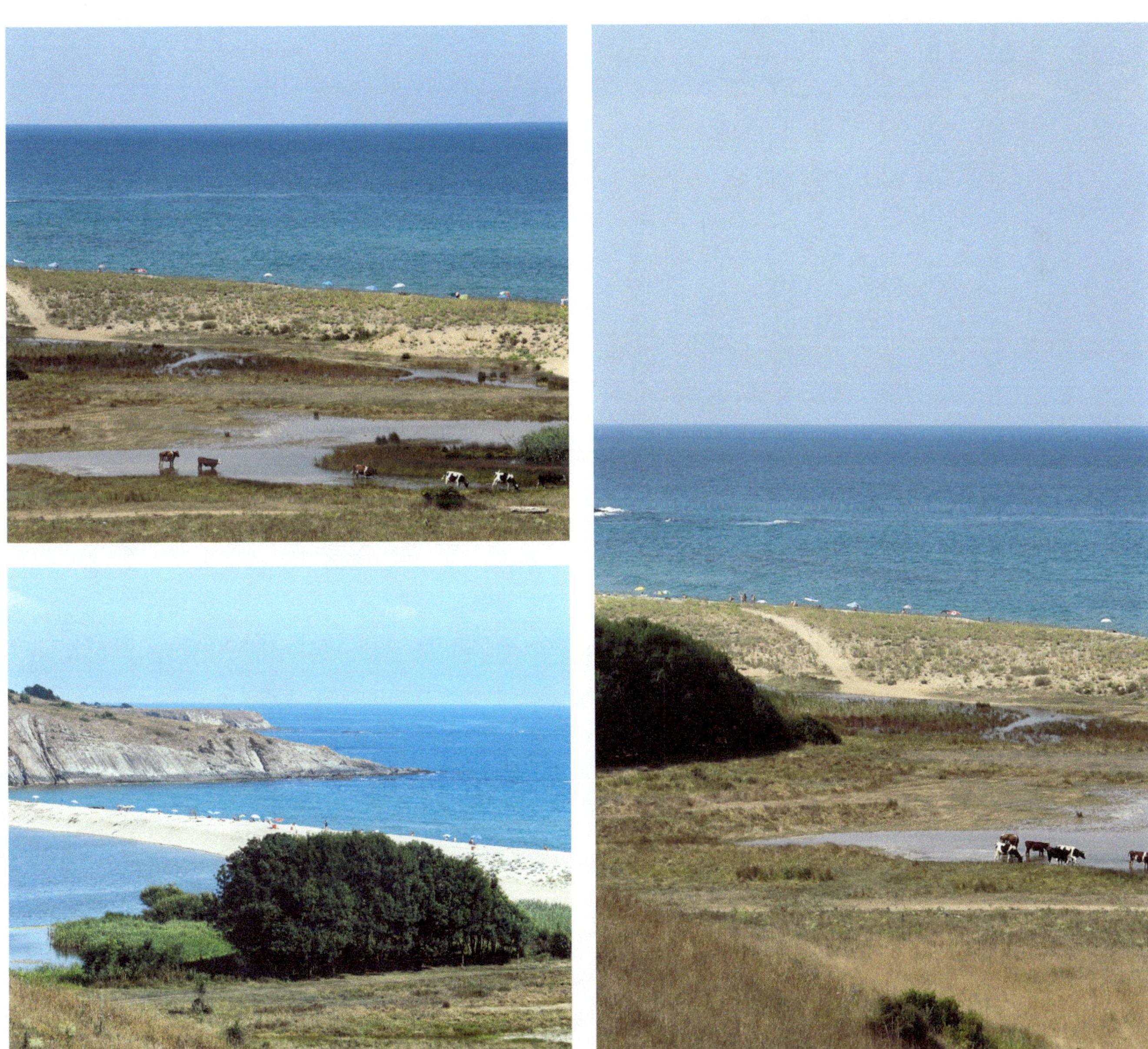

Sinemorets Bulgaria

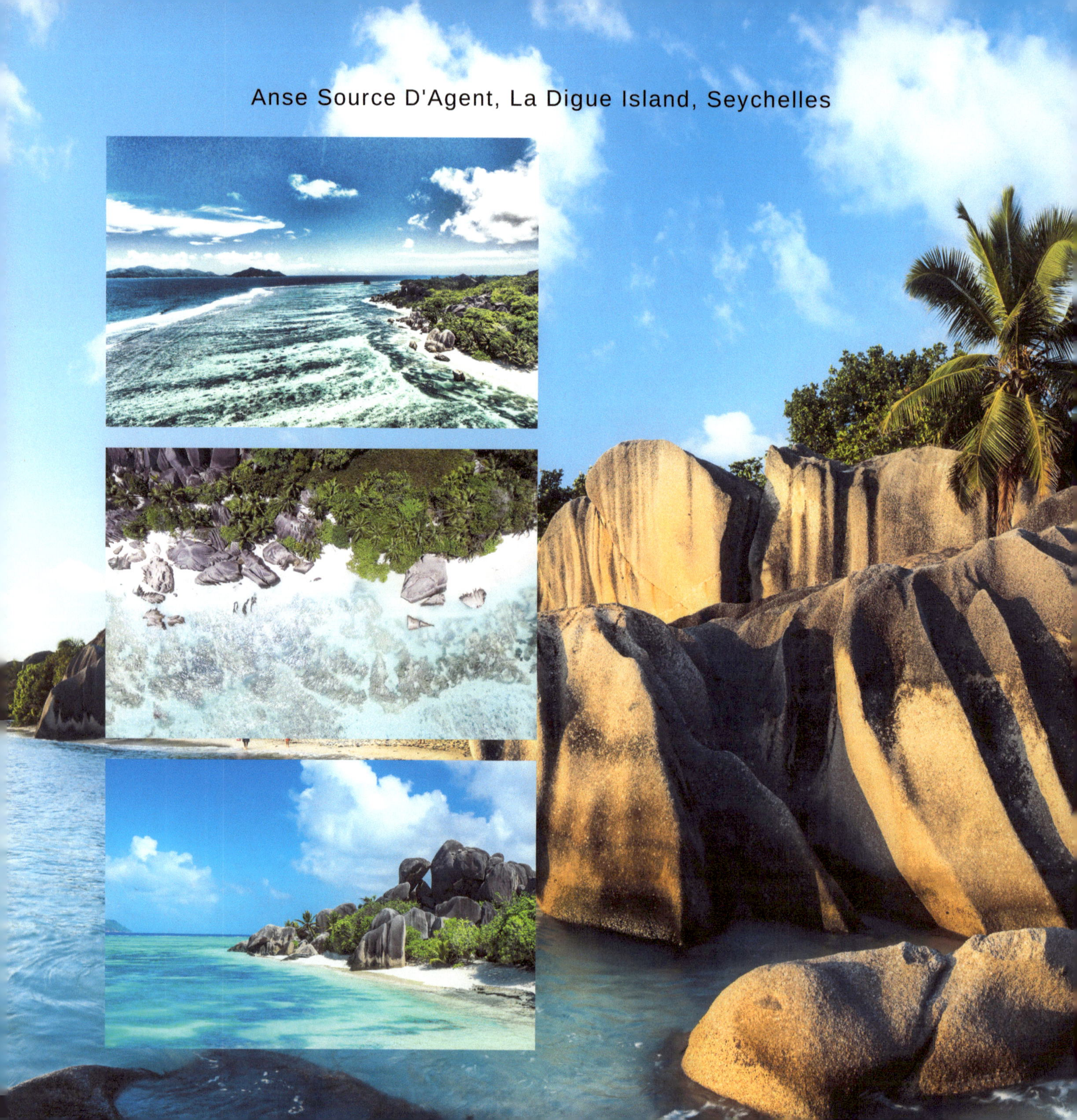

Anse Source D'Agent, La Digue Island, Seychelles

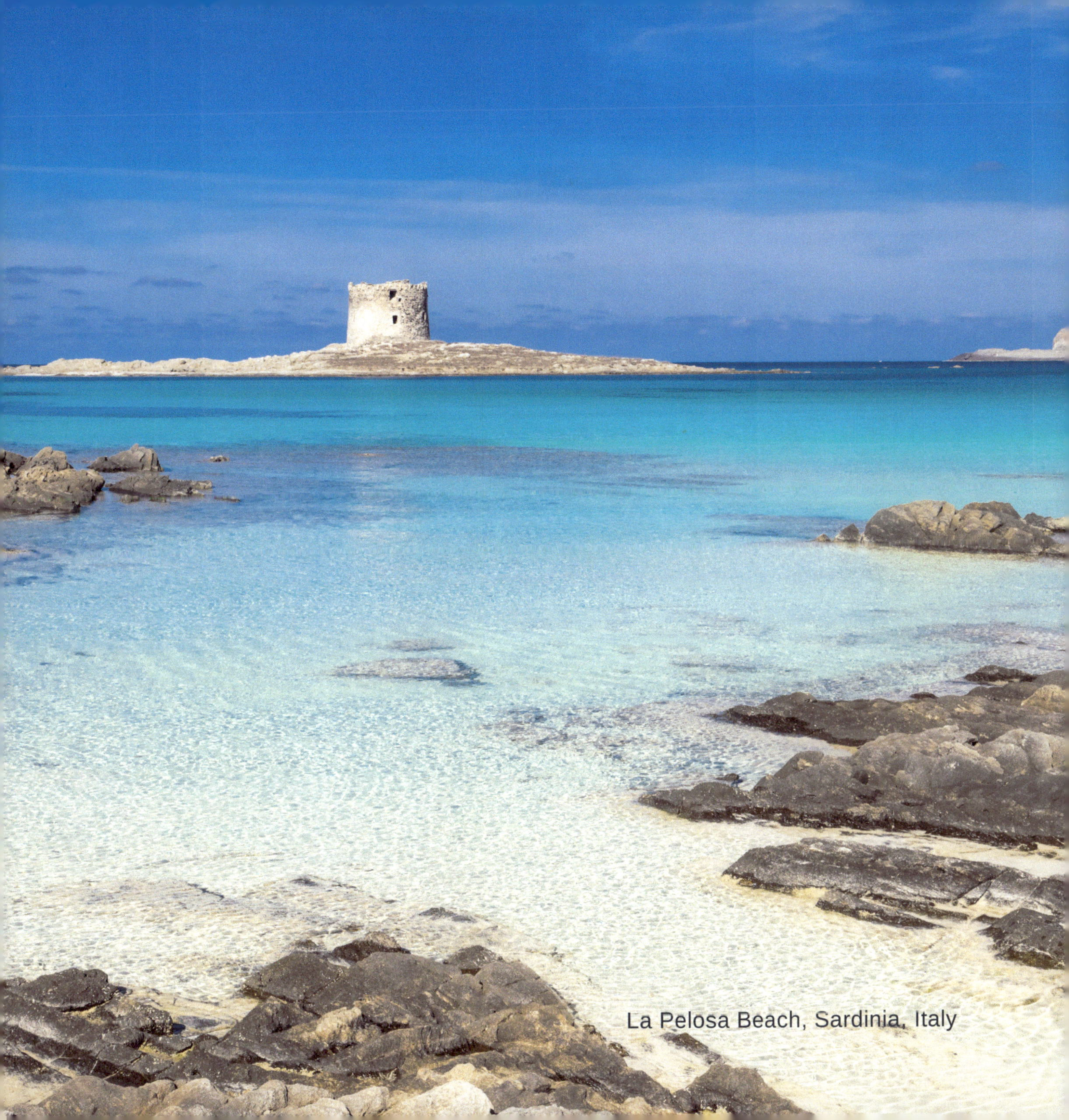

La Pelosa Beach, Sardinia, Italy

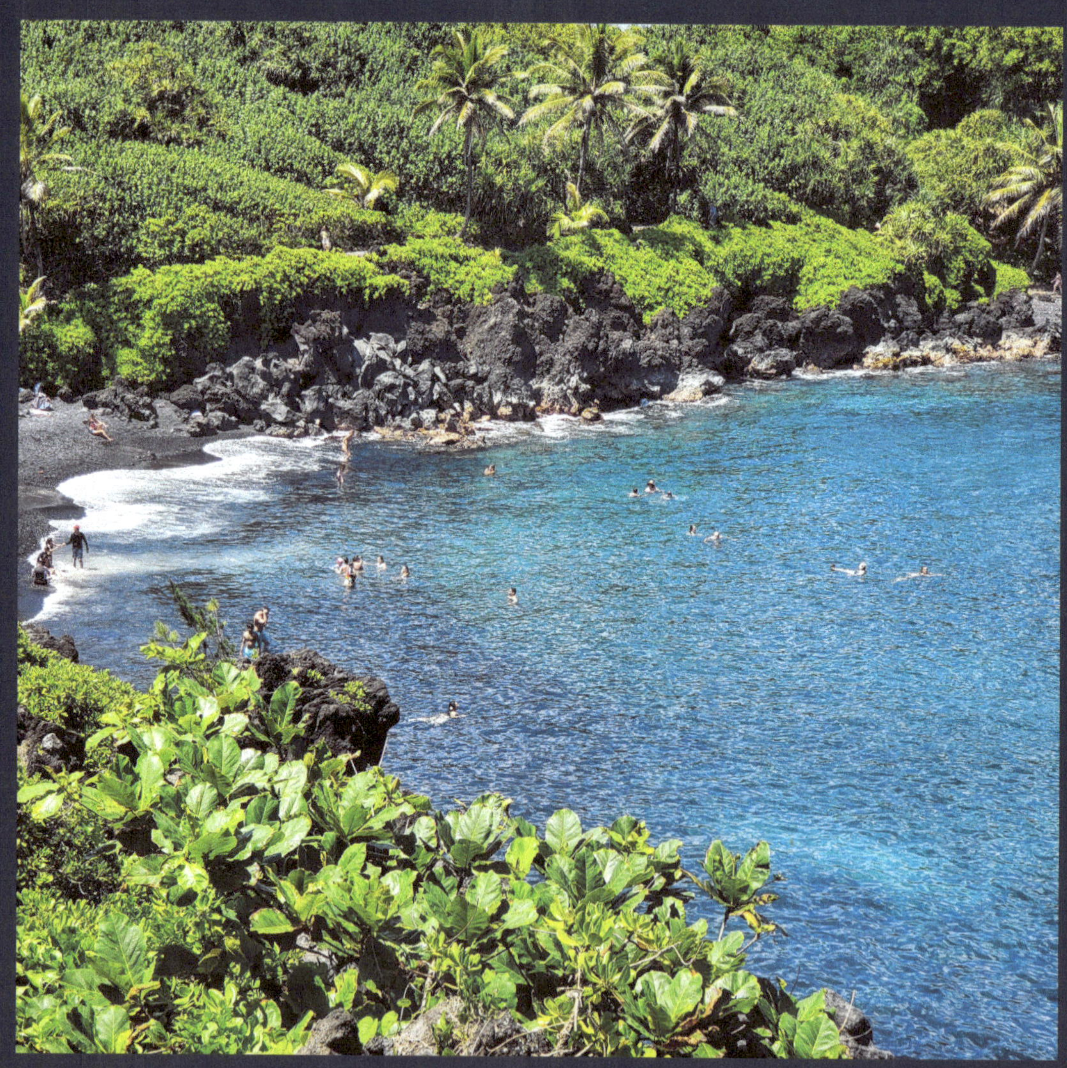

Honokalani Beach, Maui

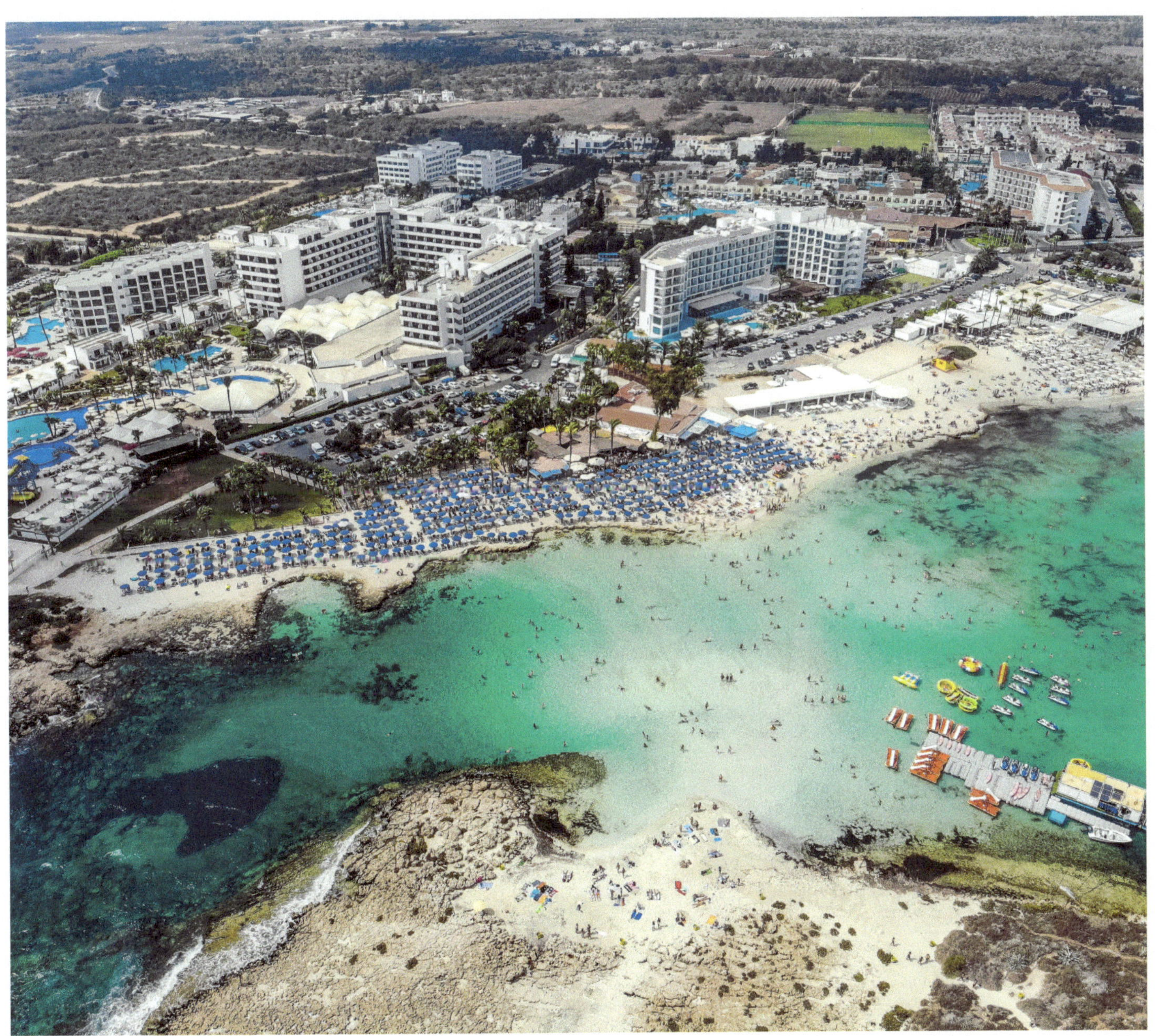

Nissi Beach , Cyprus

Bowman's Beach, Sanibel Island

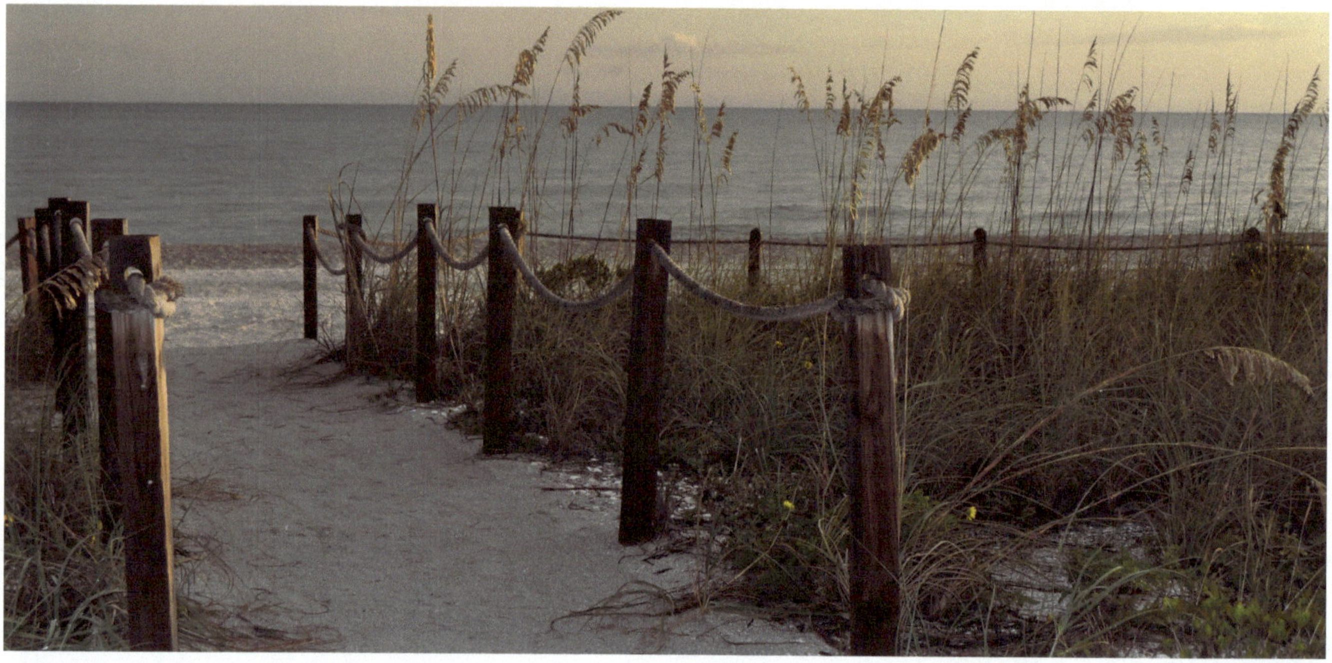

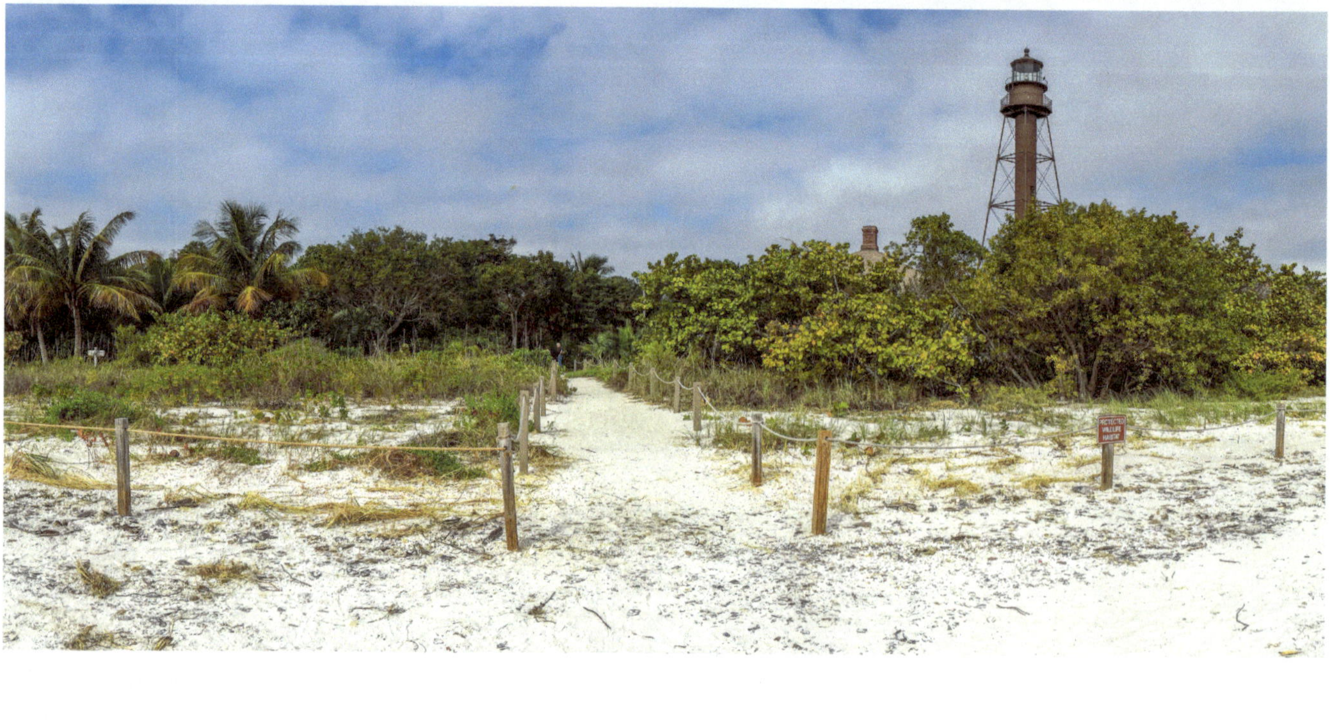

Pensacola Beach, Florida

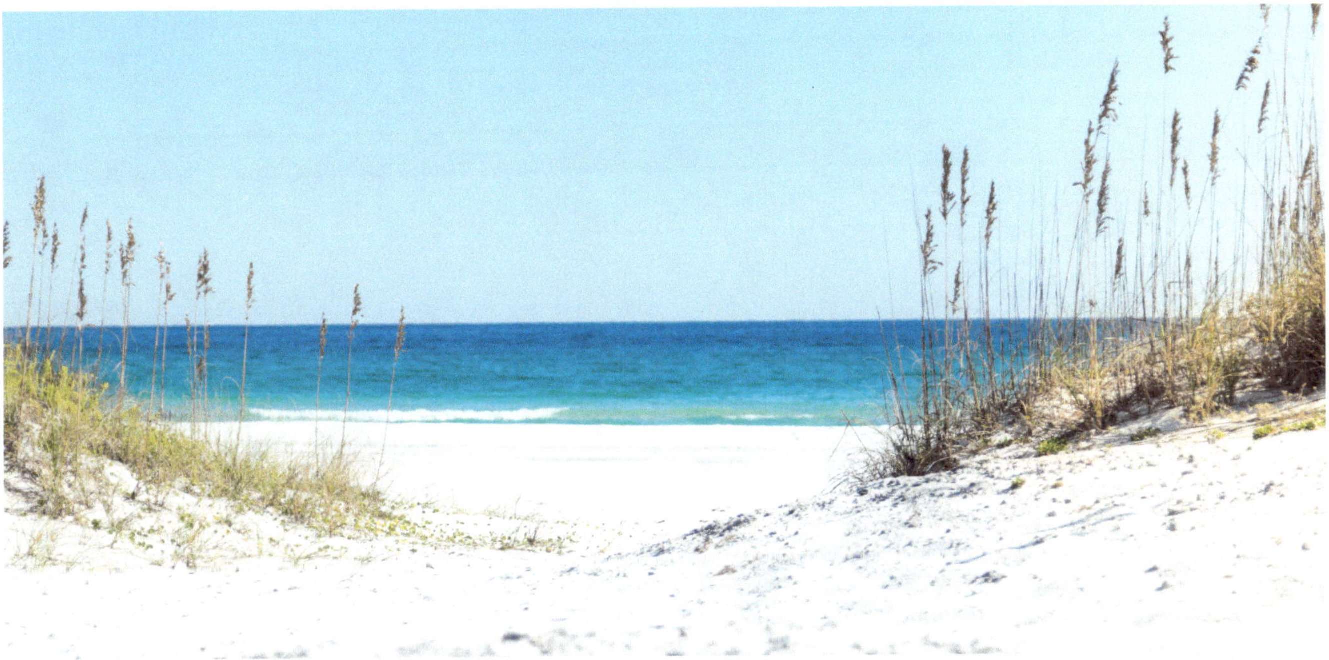

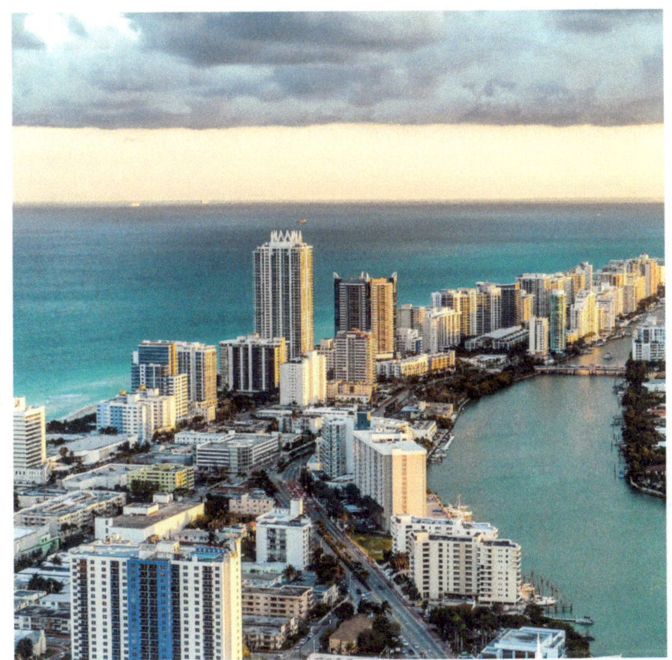

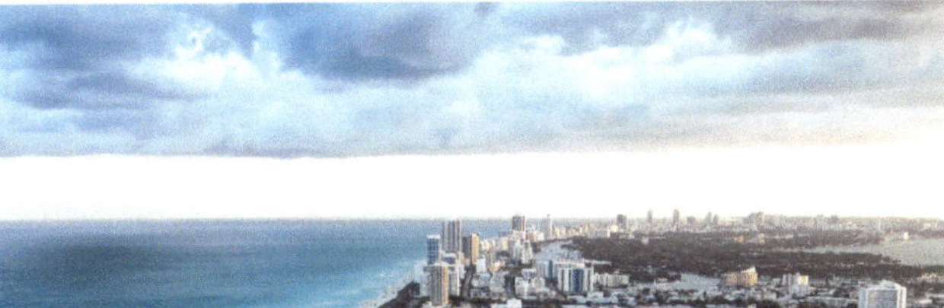

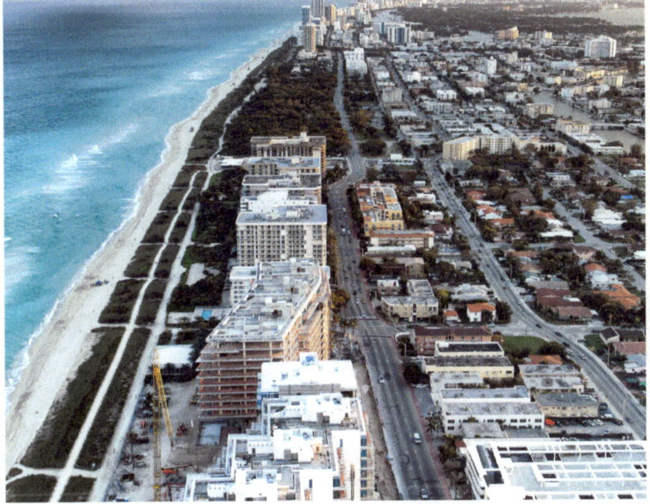

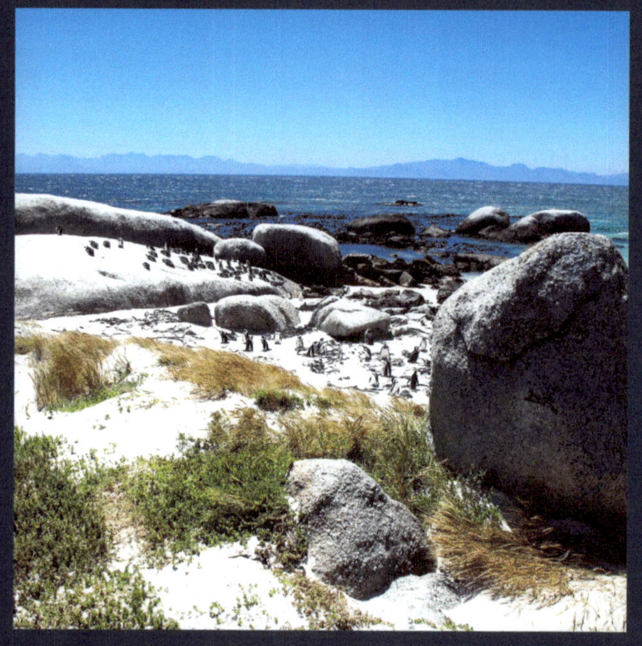

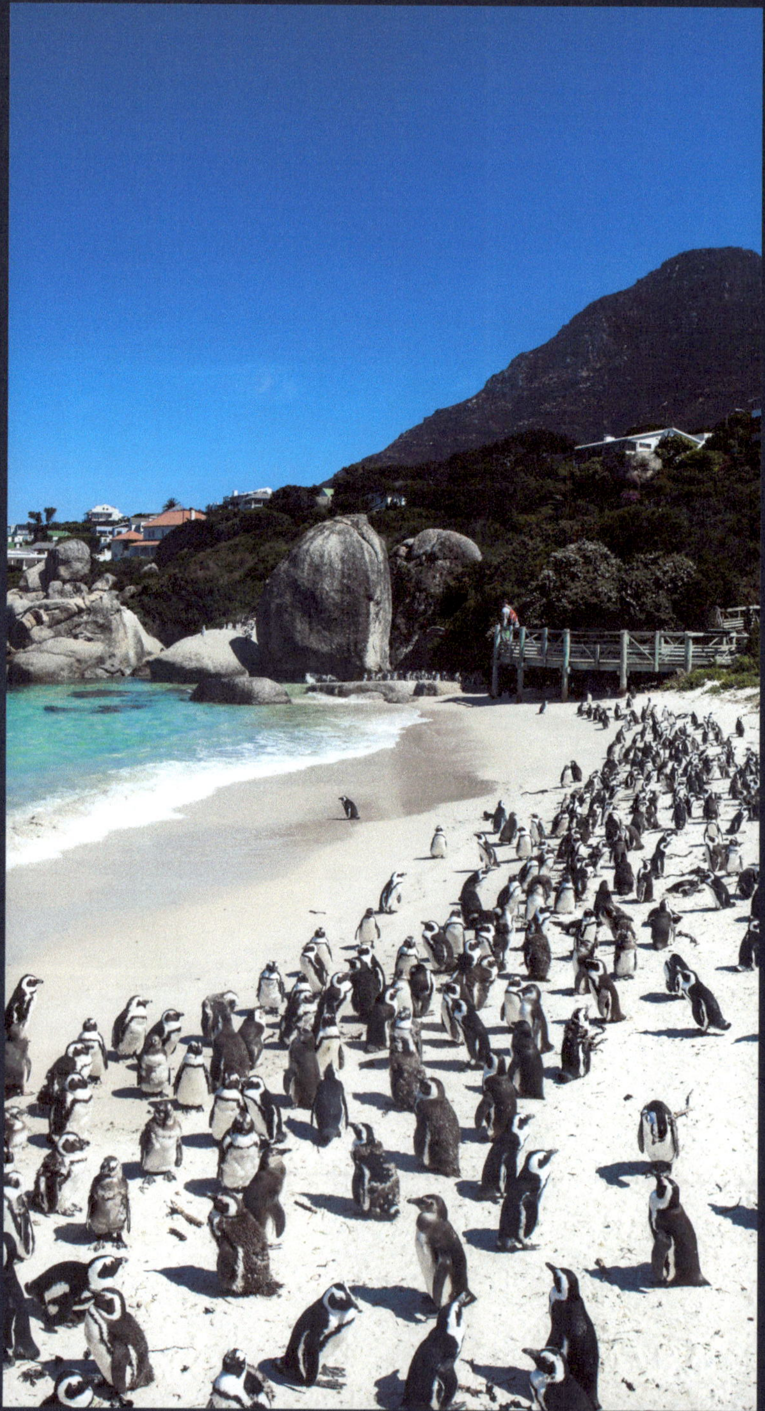

Boulders Beach, South Africa

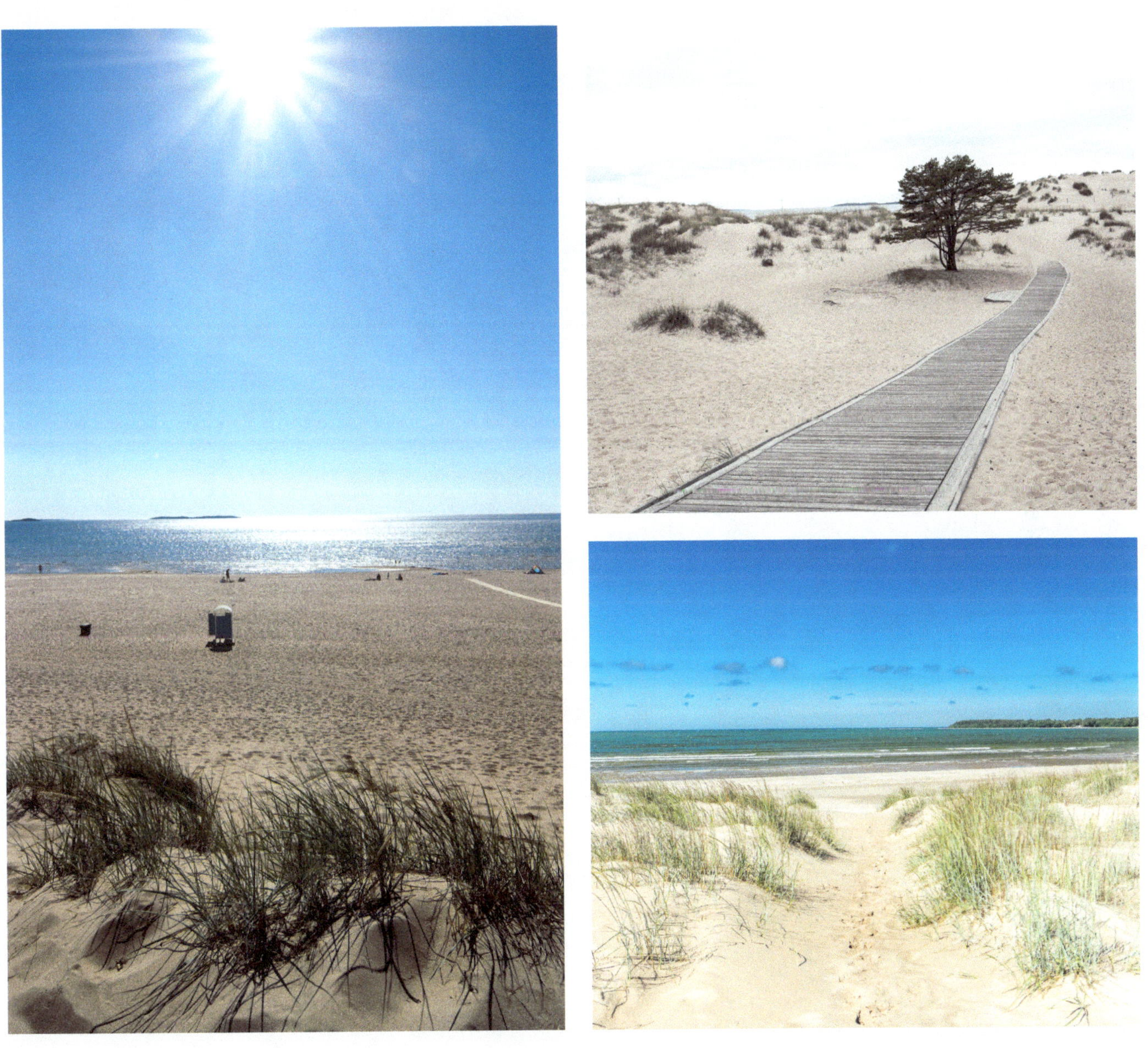

Yyteri Beach, Finland

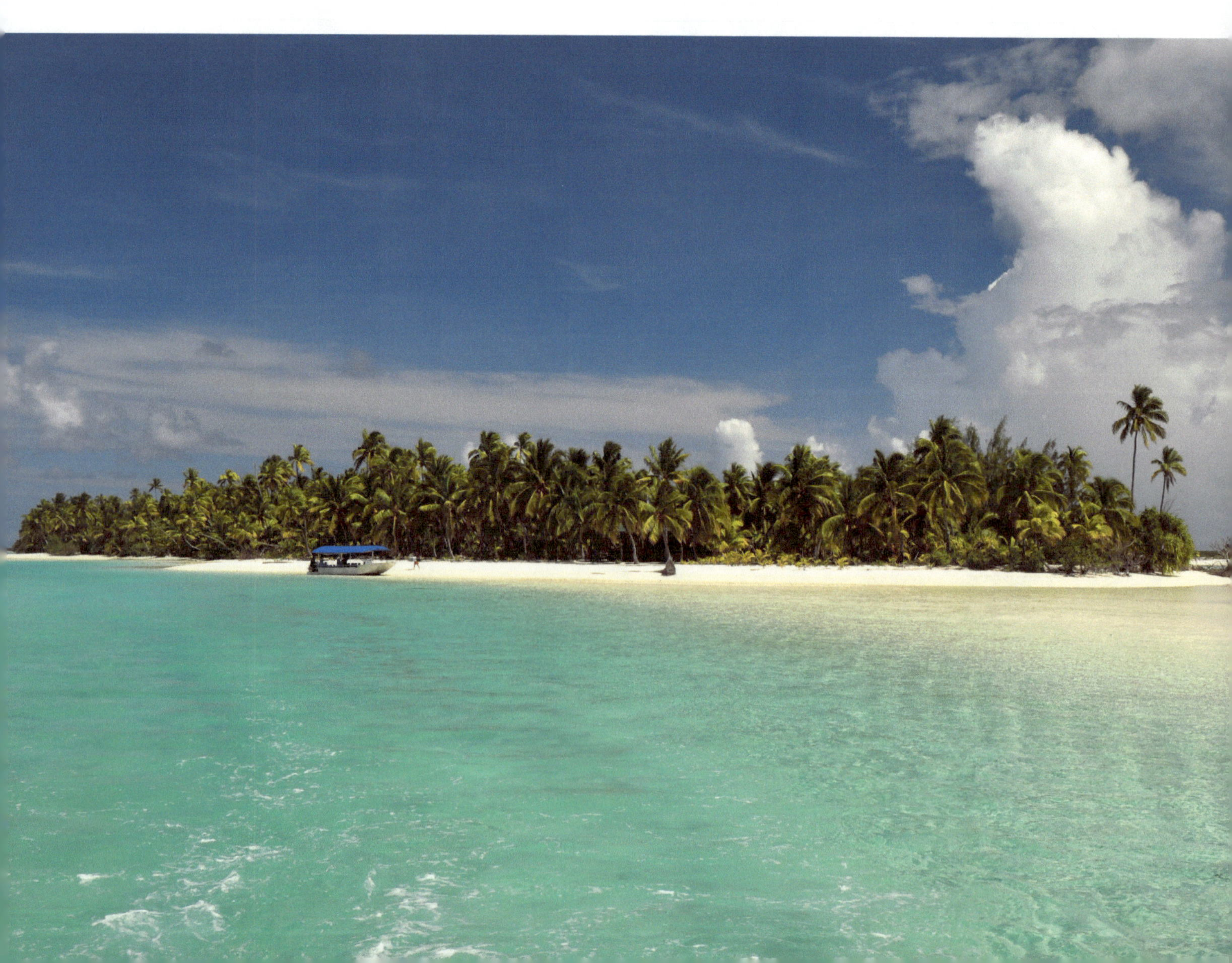

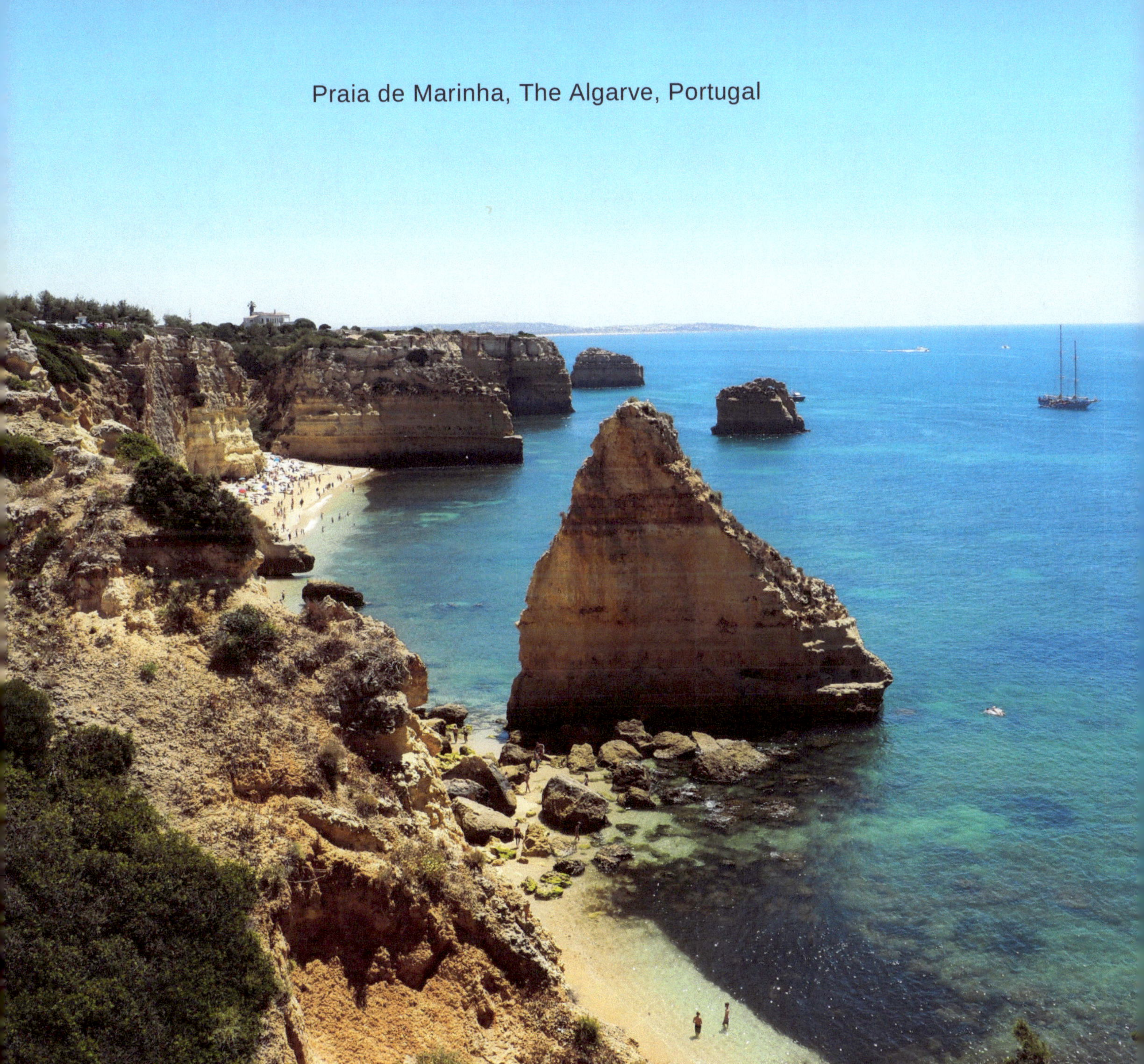
Praia de Marinha, The Algarve, Portugal

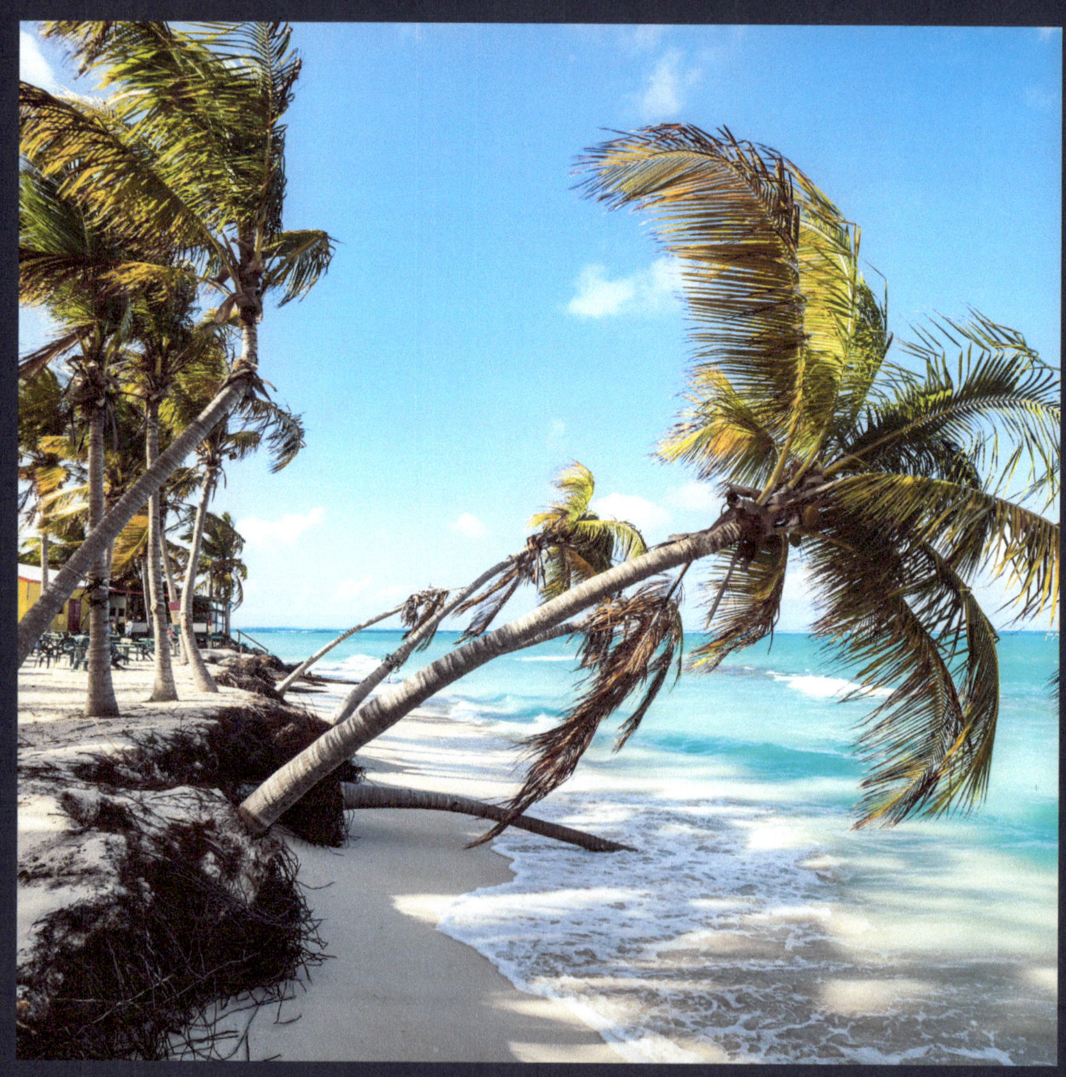

Shoal Bay, Anguilla

Long Beach, Vancouver island

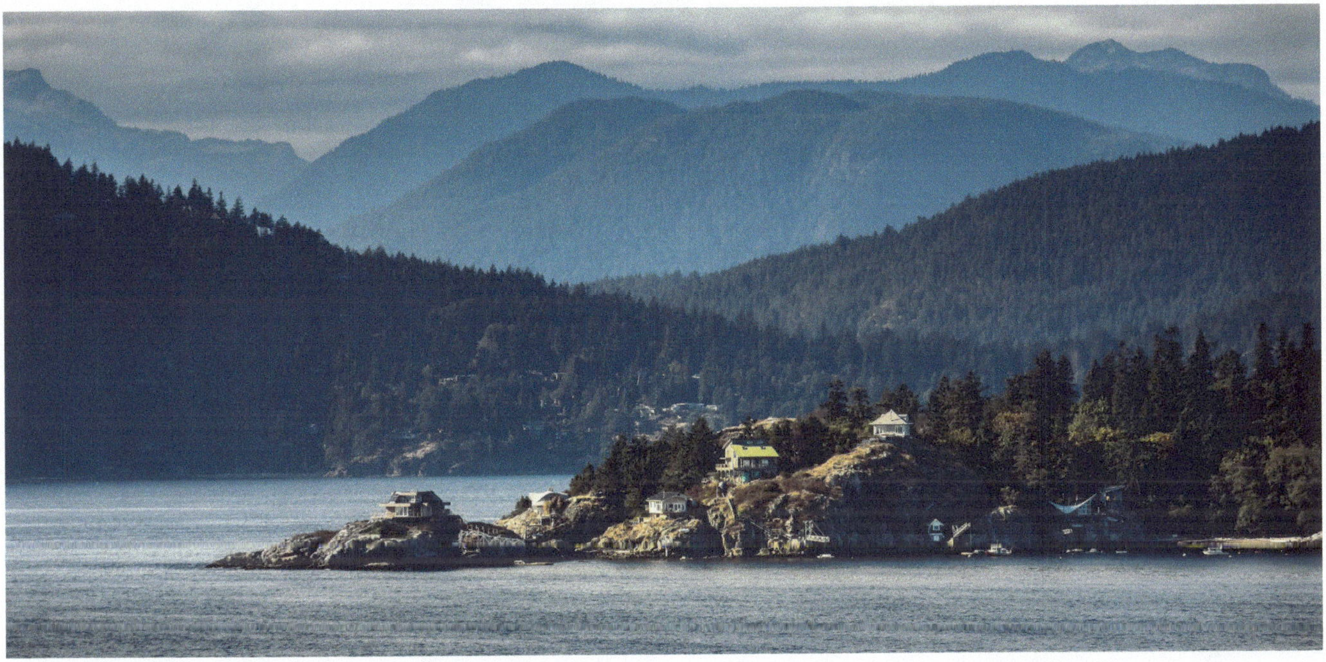

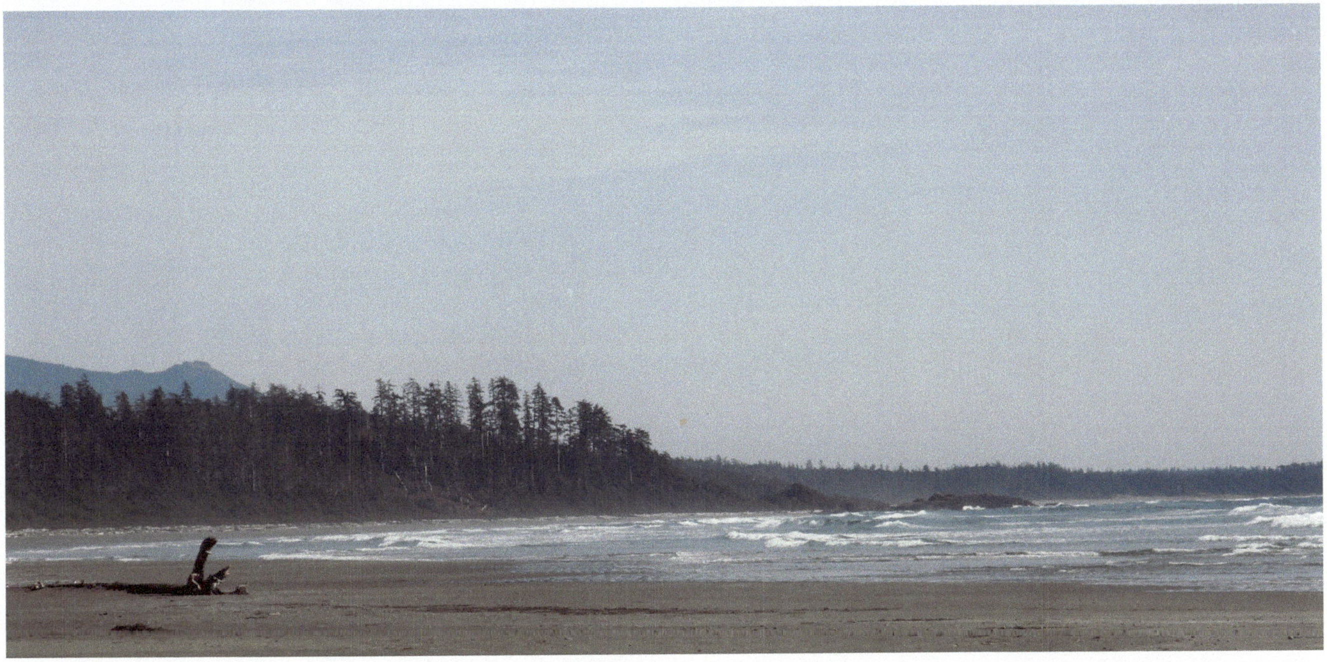

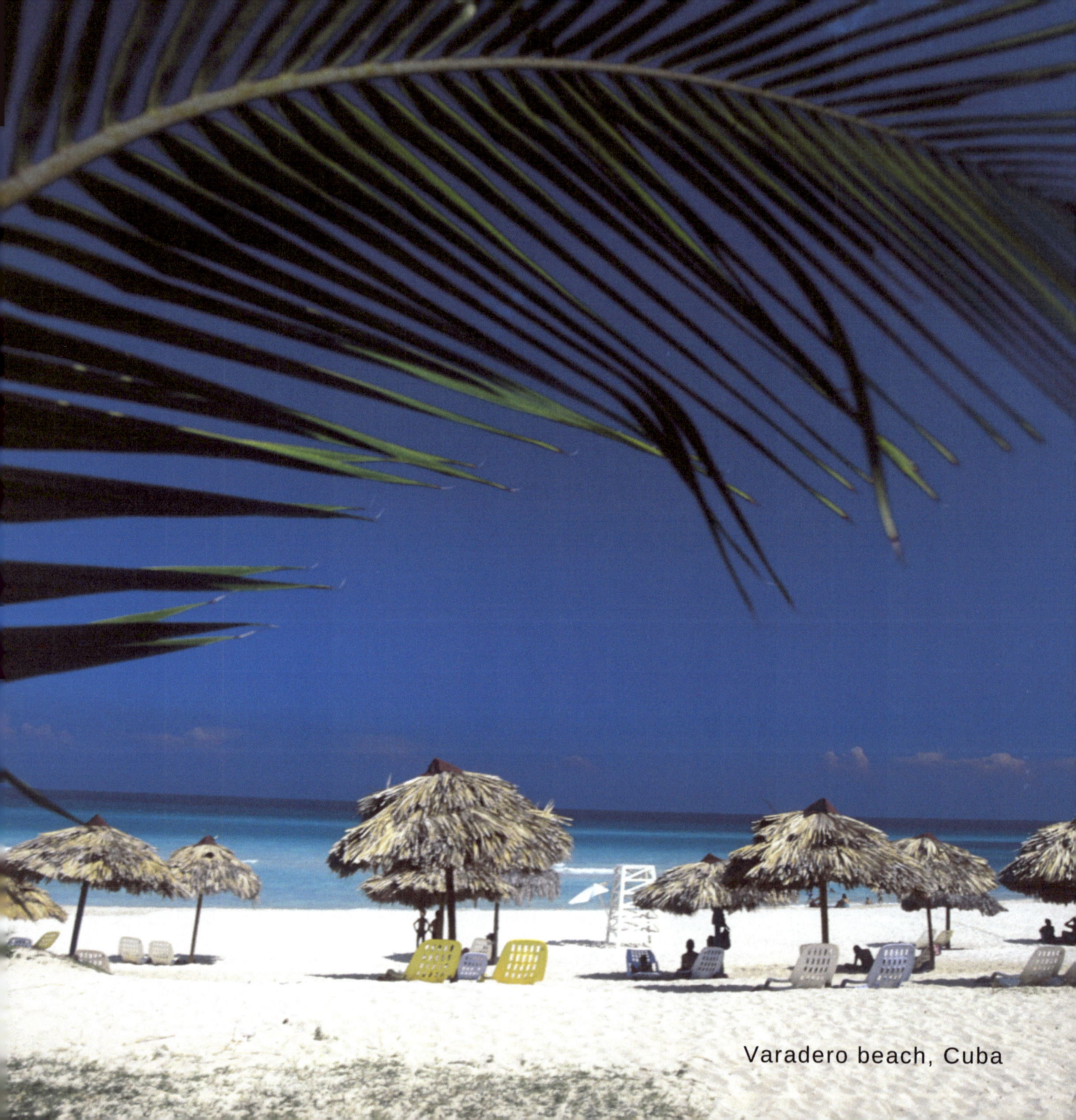

Varadero beach, Cuba

Bondi Beach, Australia

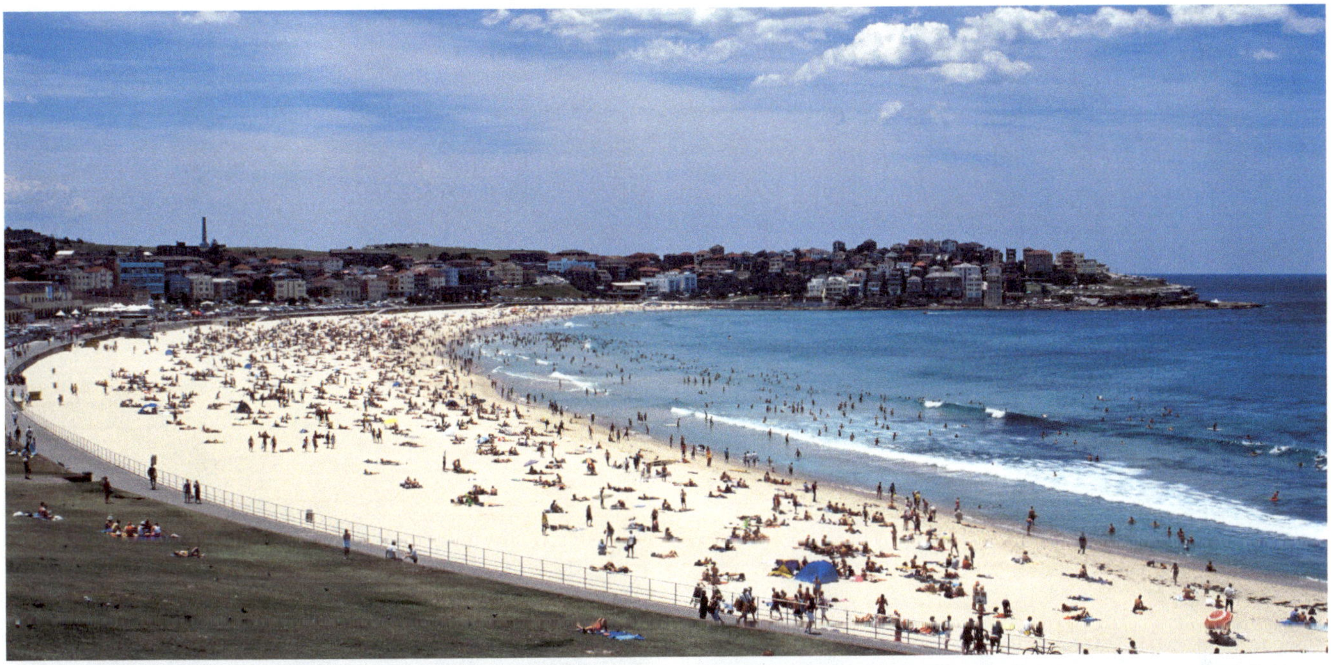

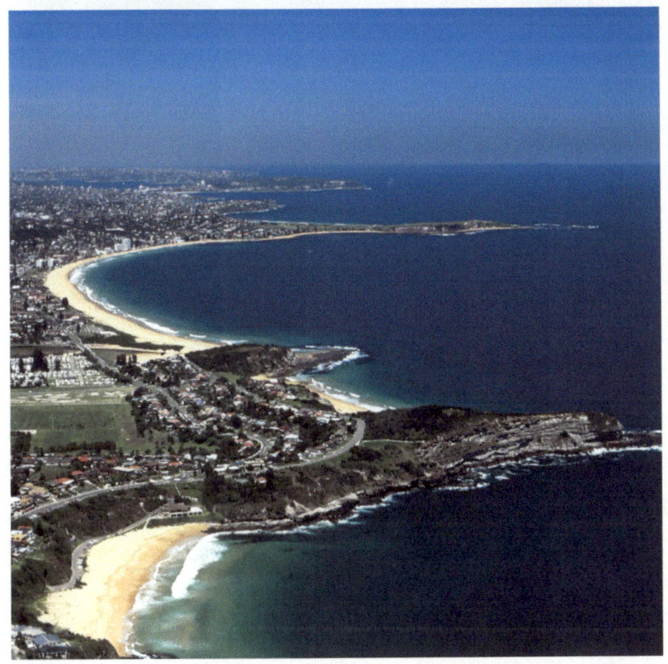 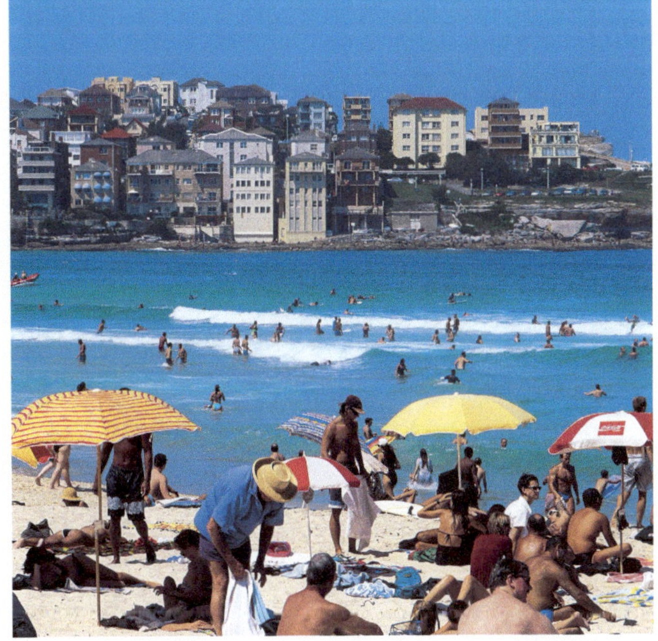

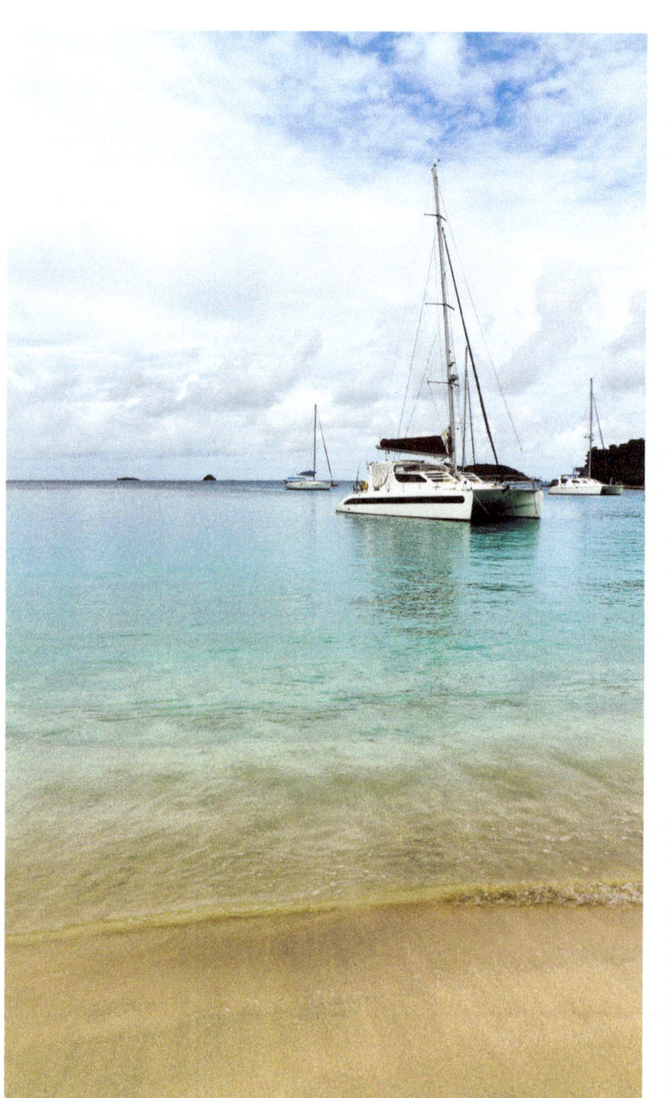 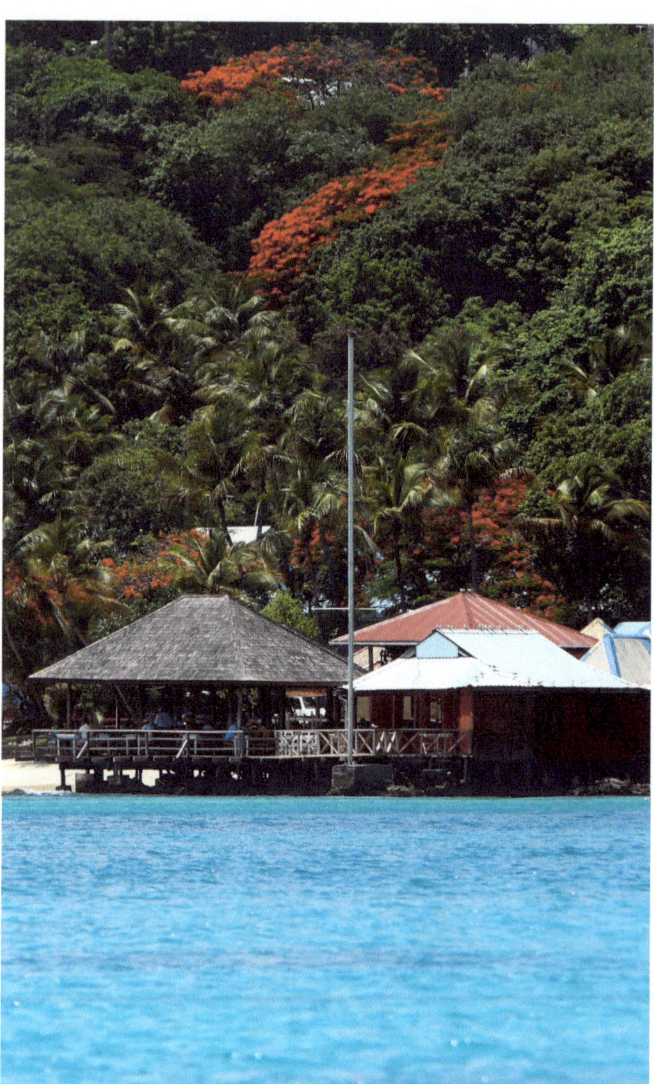

Saltwhistle Bay, St. Vincent and Grenadines

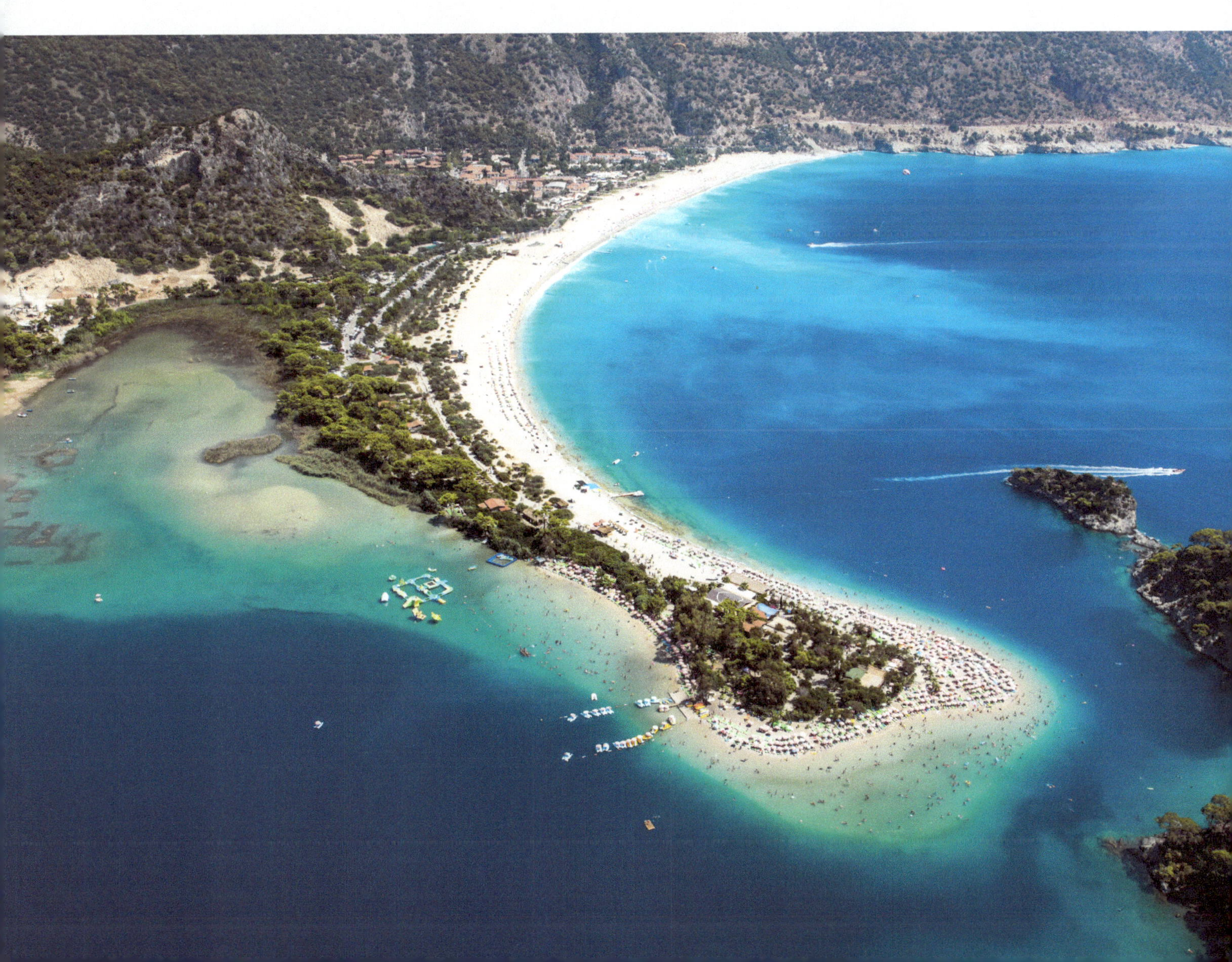

Blue Lagoon, Fiji

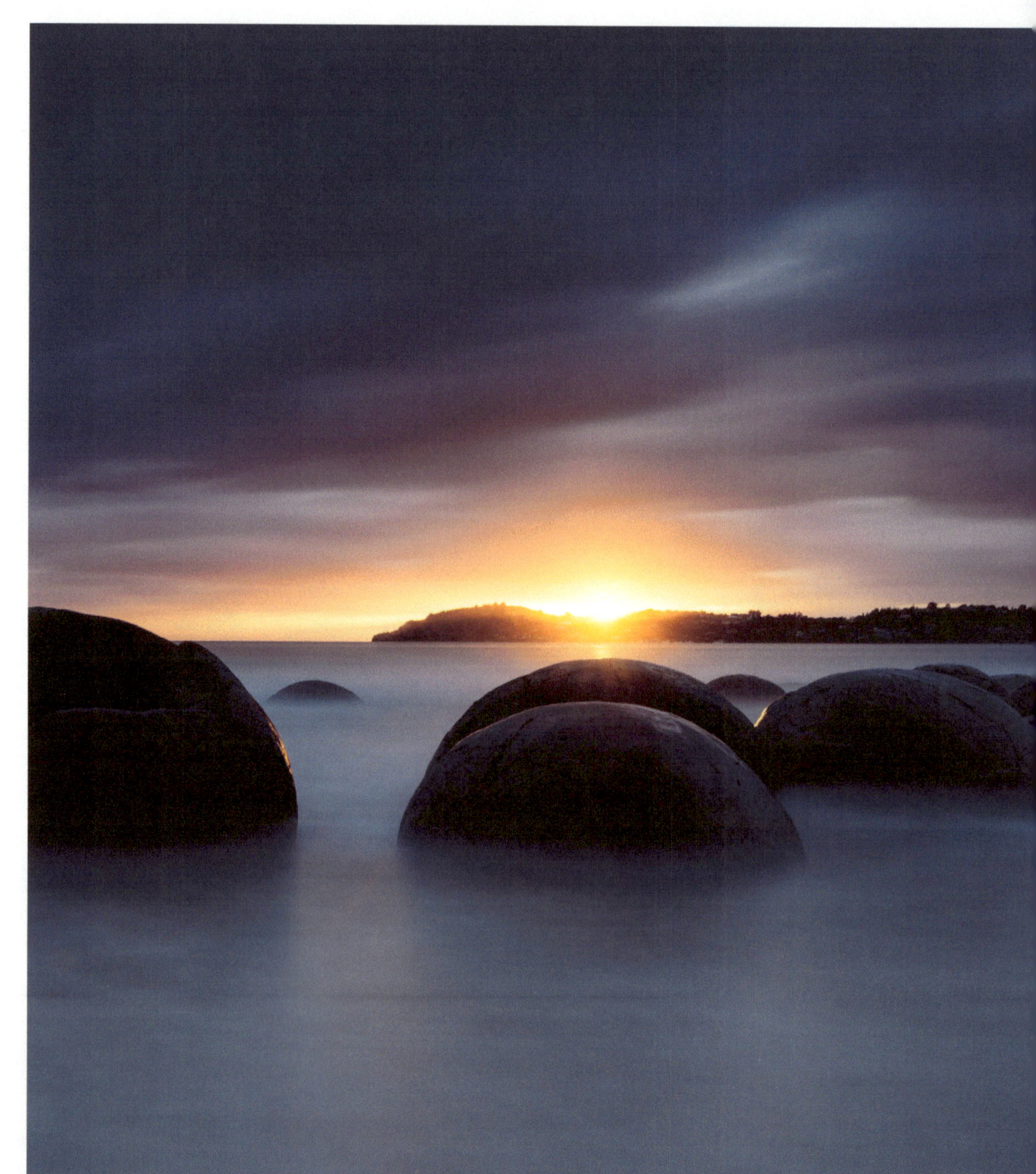

Koekohe Beach
– New Zealand

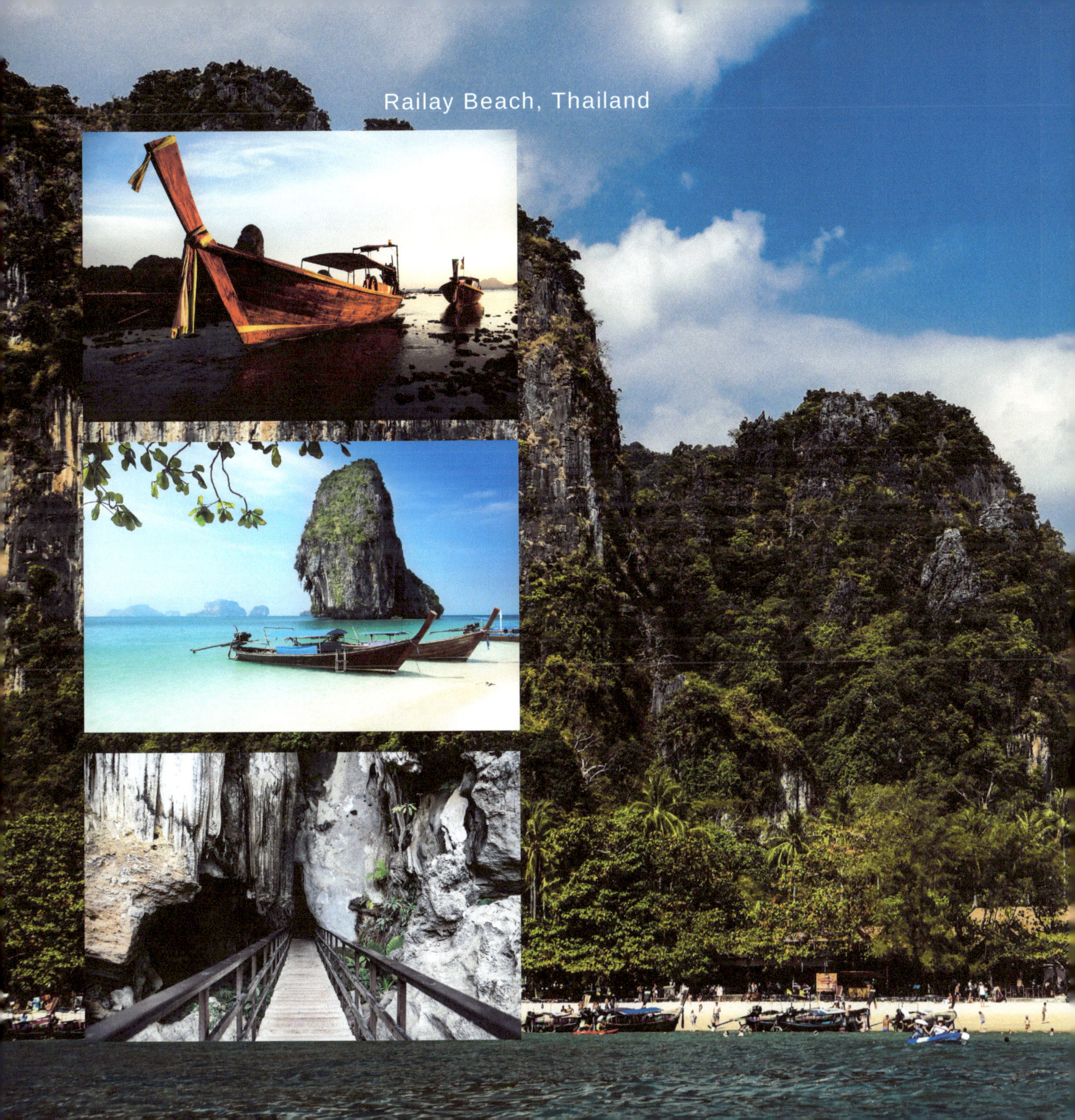

Railay Beach, Thailand

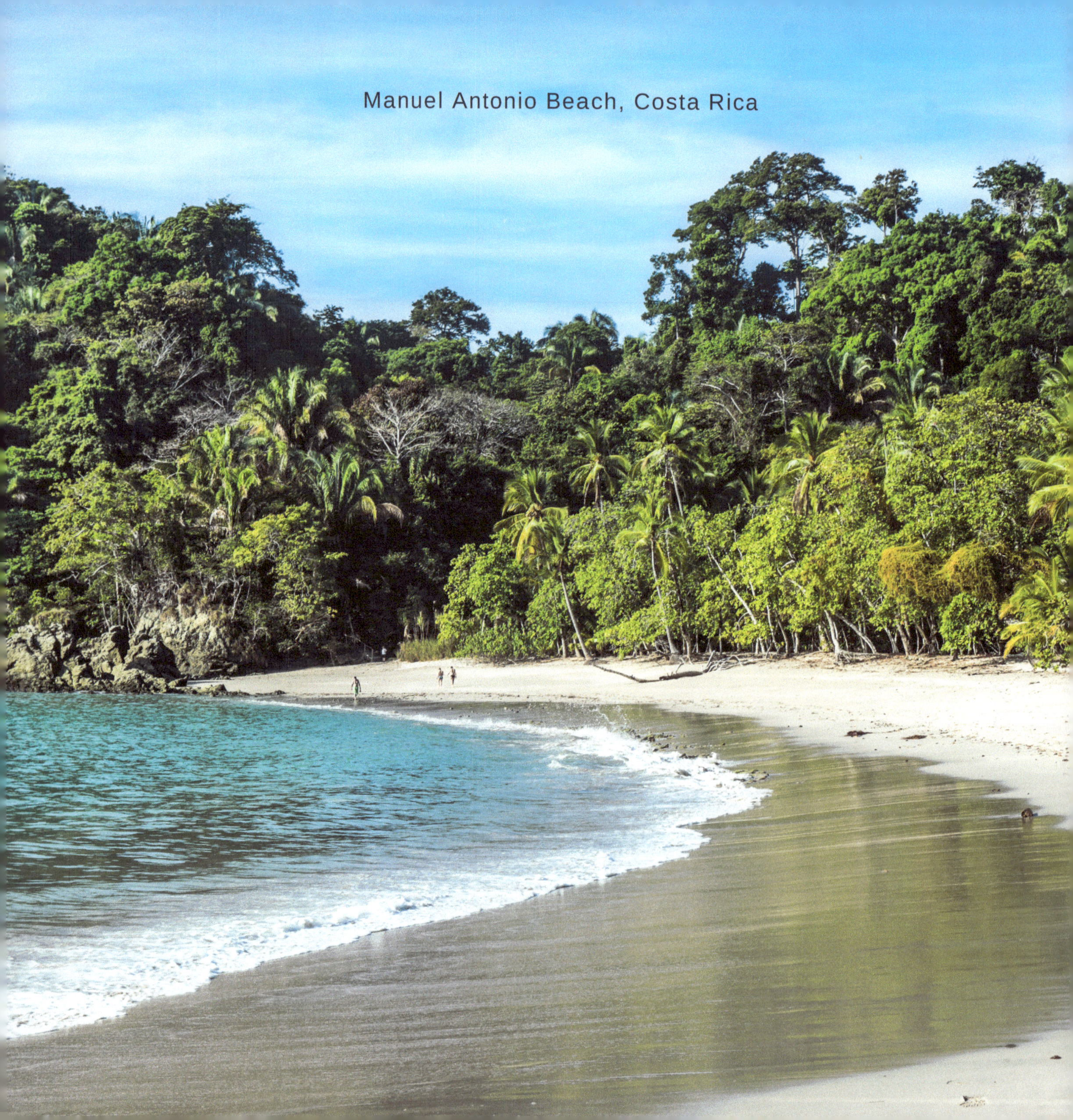
Manuel Antonio Beach, Costa Rica

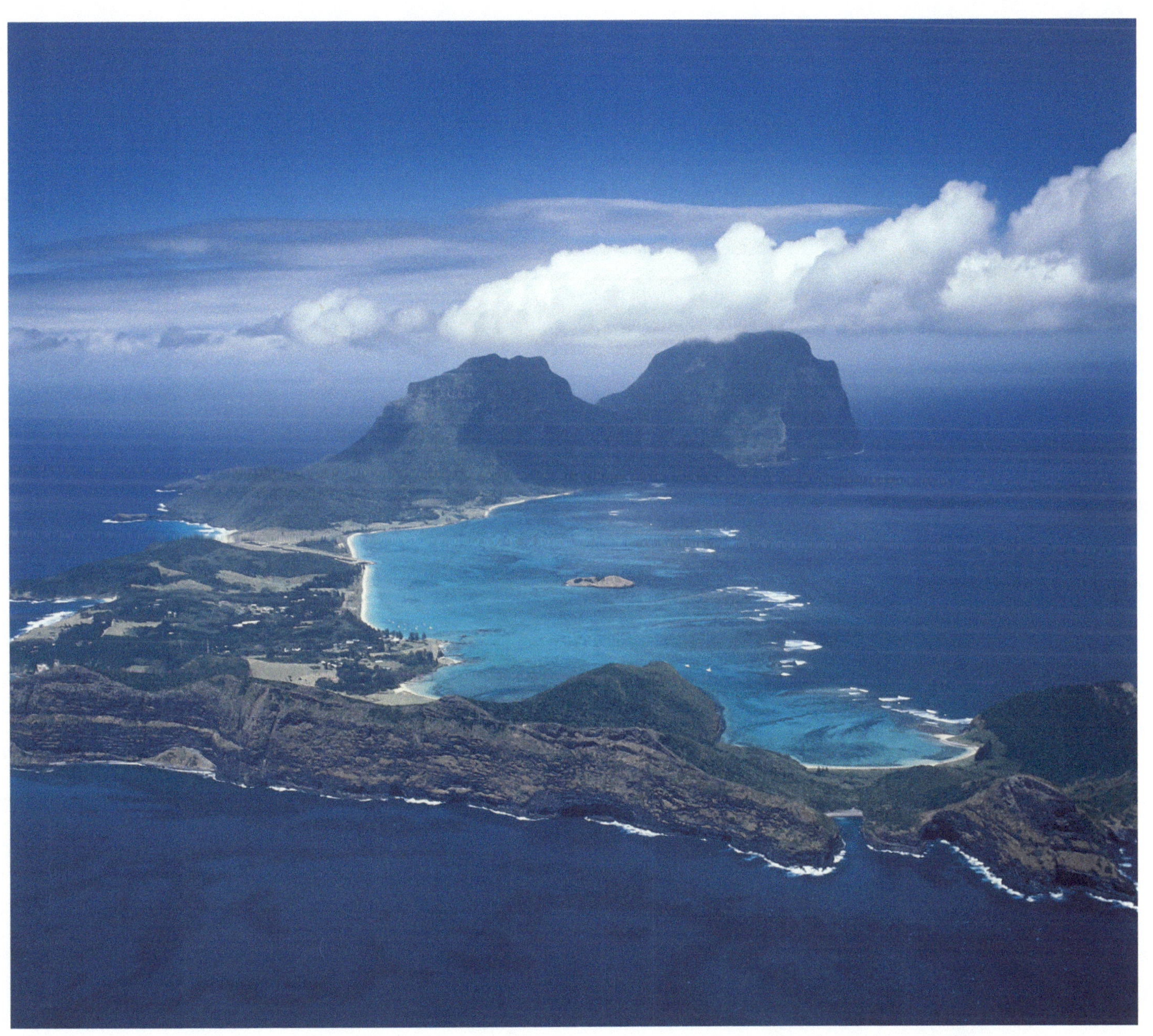

Blinky Beach, Lord Howe Island

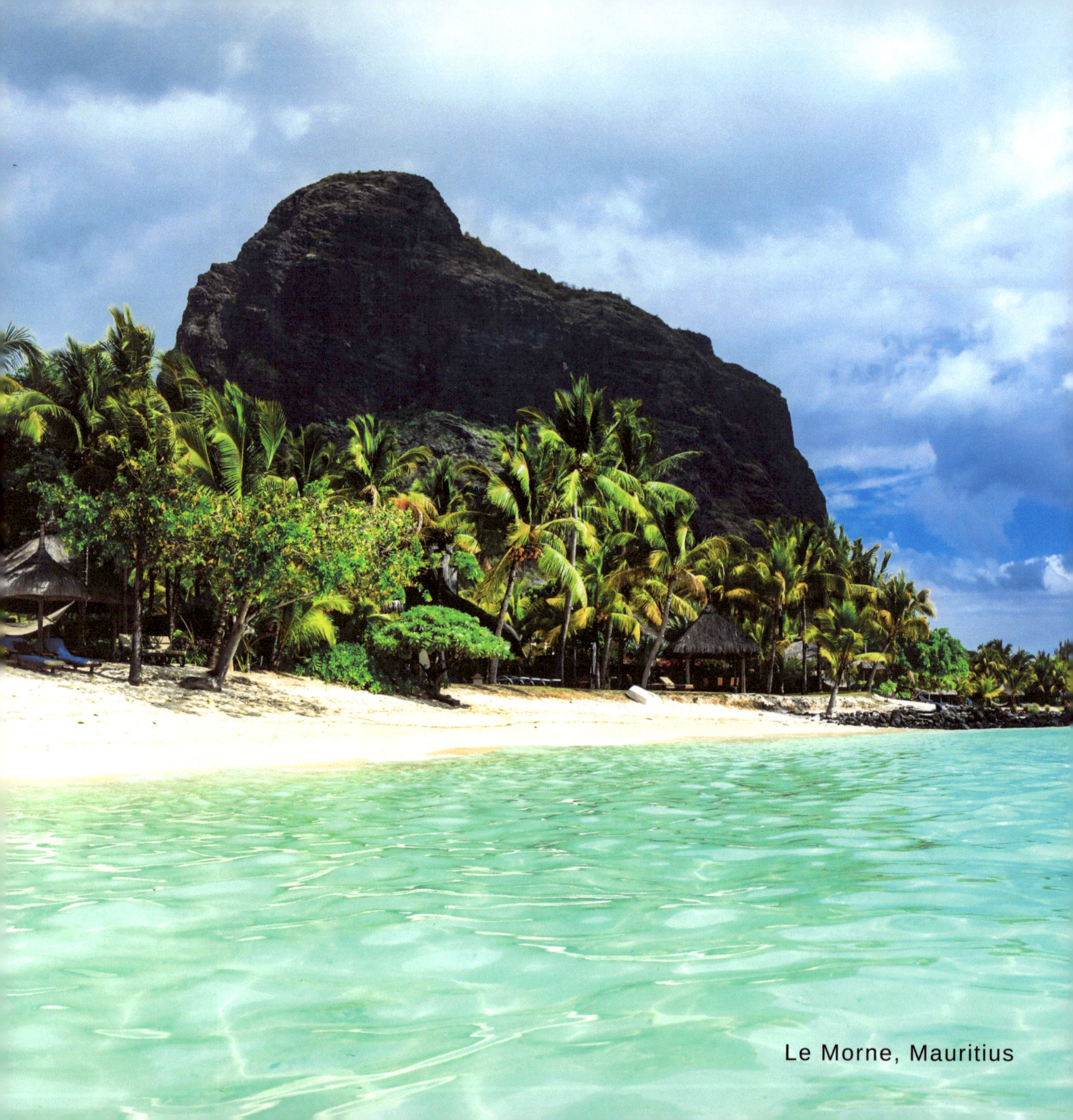

Le Morne, Mauritius

Ora Beach, Indonesia

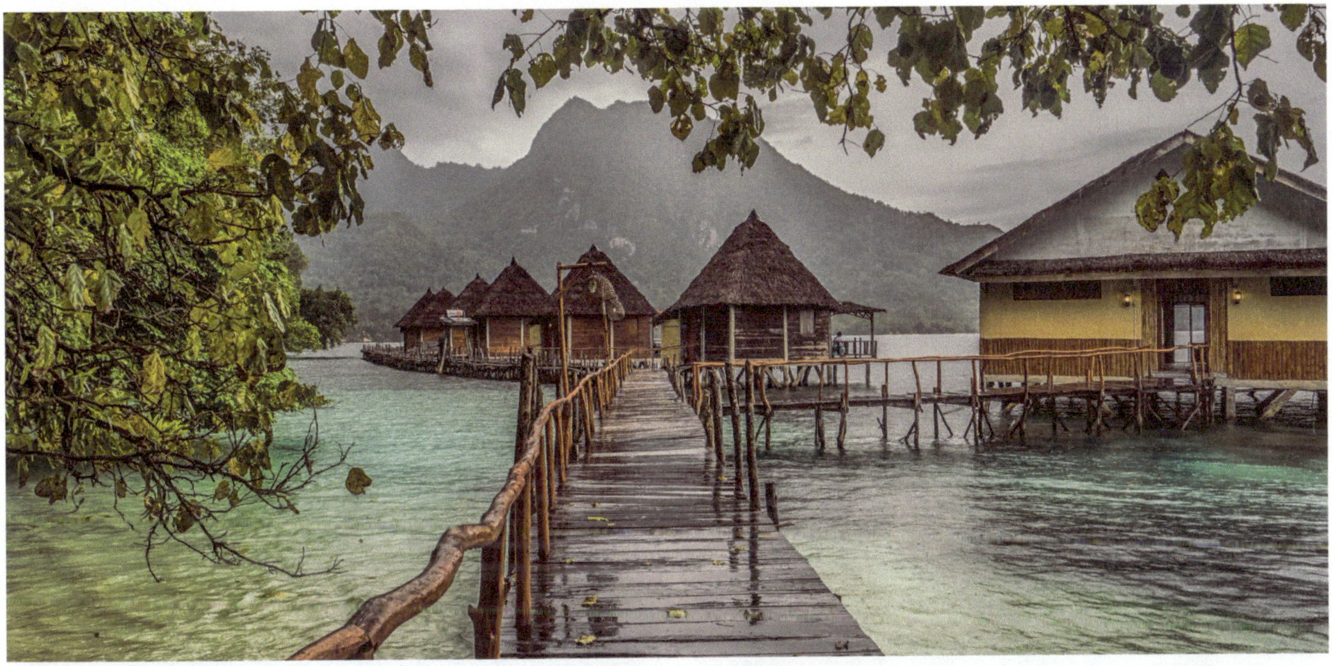

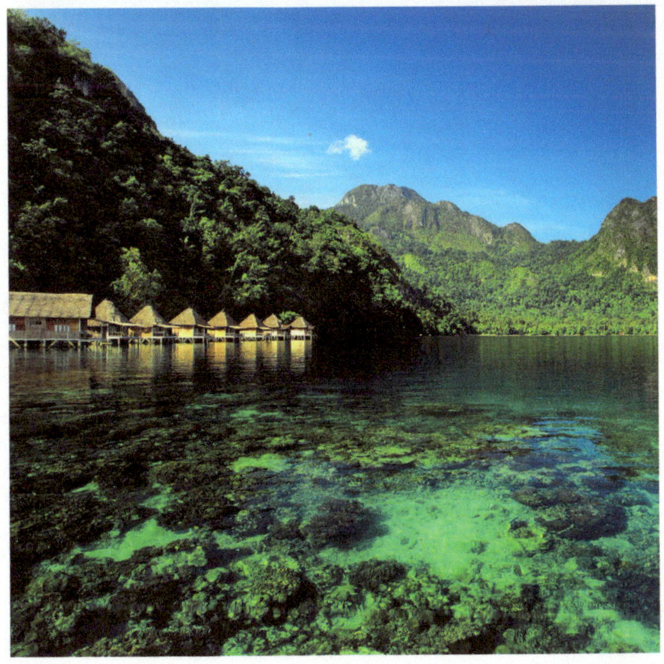

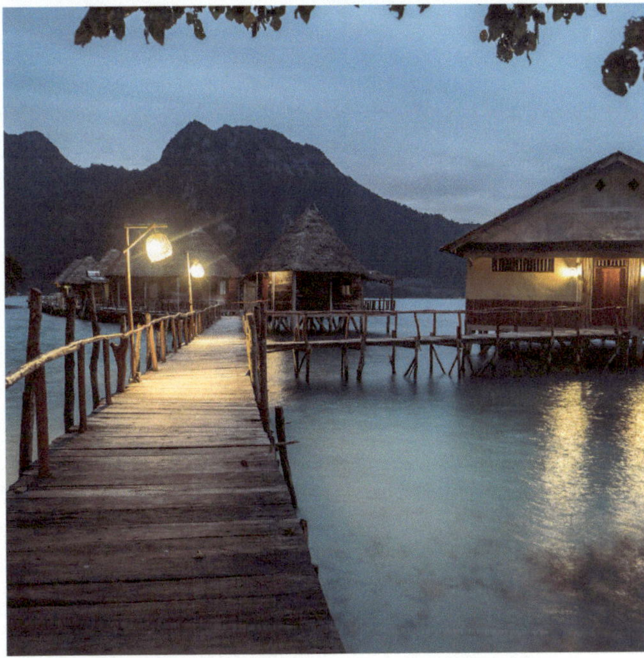

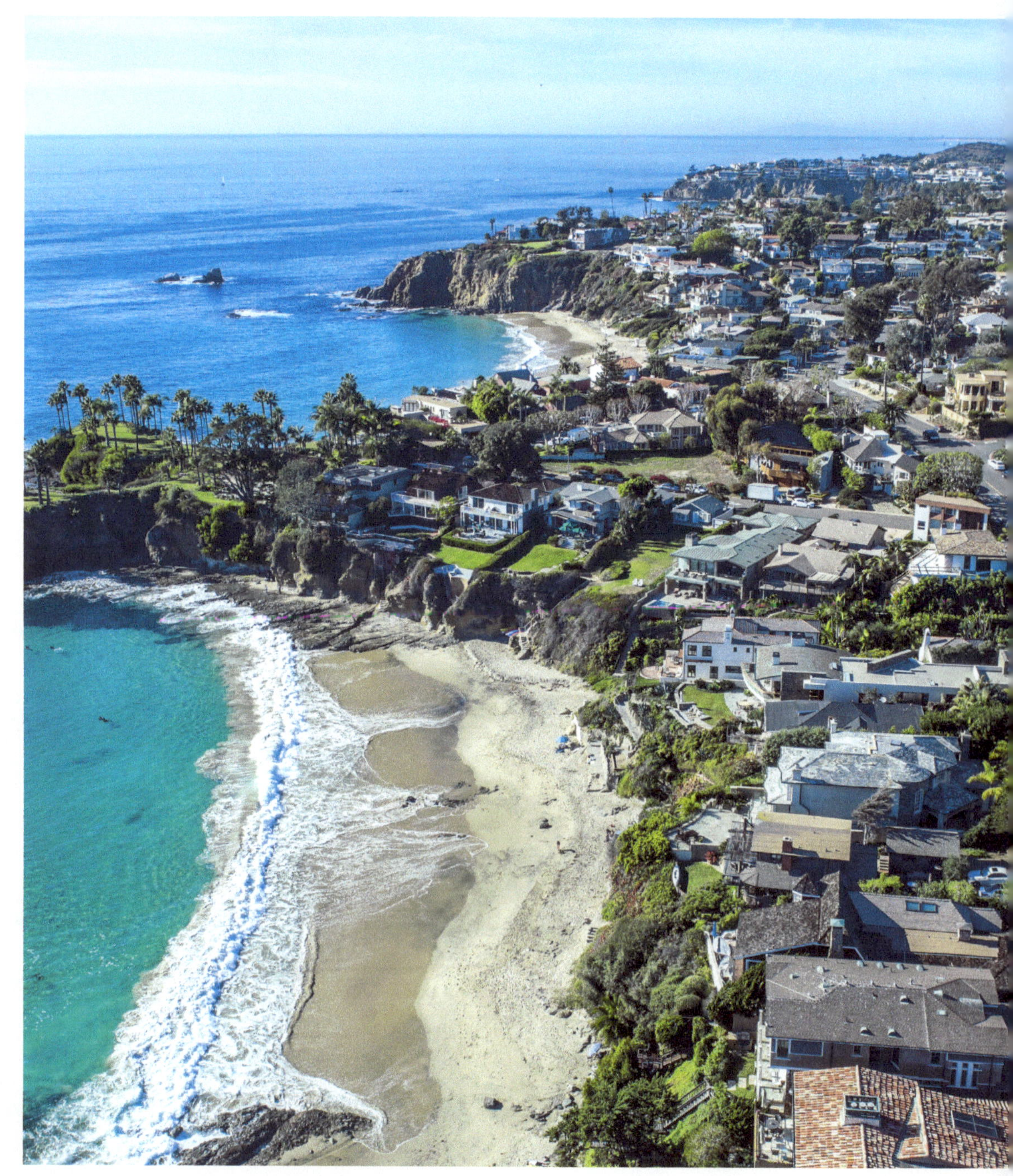

Laguna beach
USA

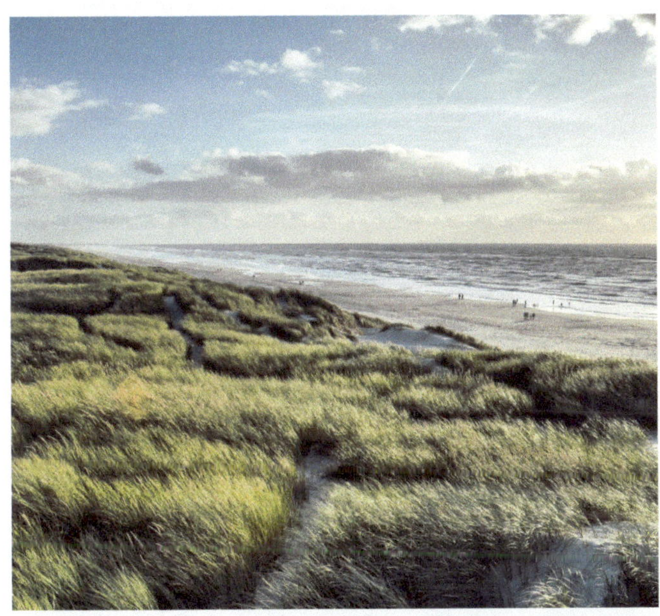
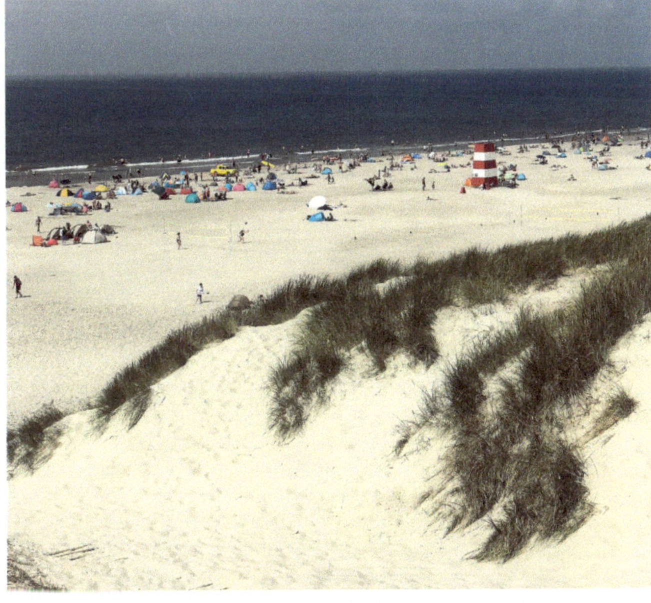
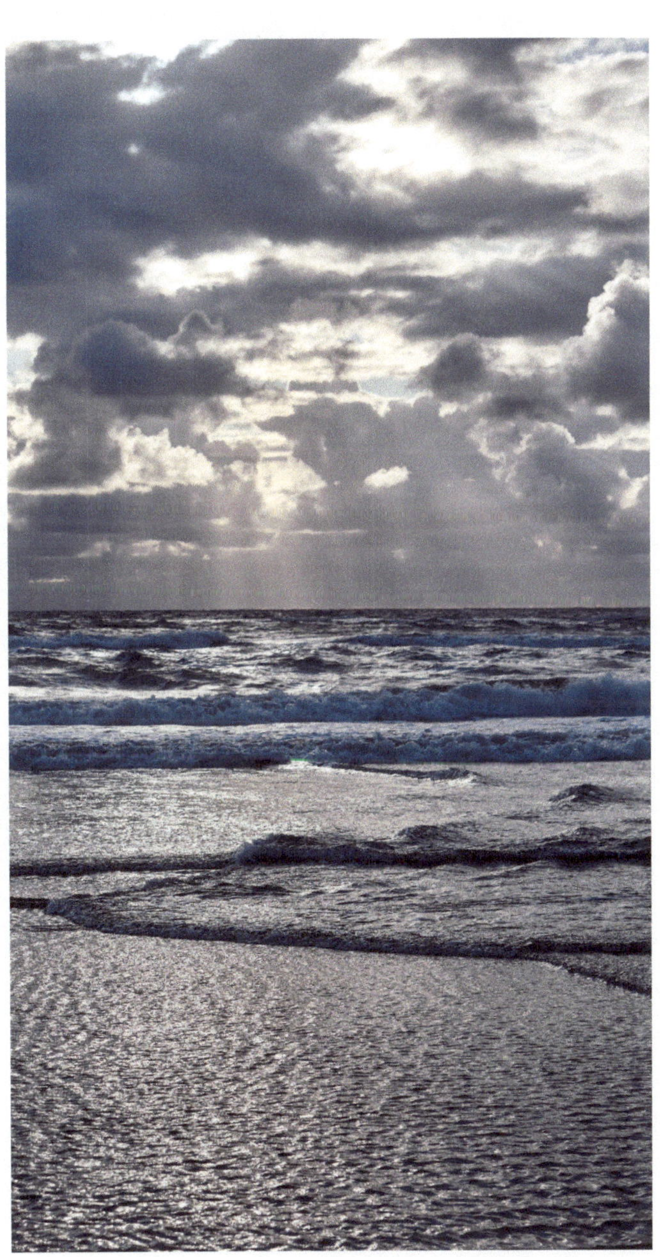

Henne Strand, Denmark

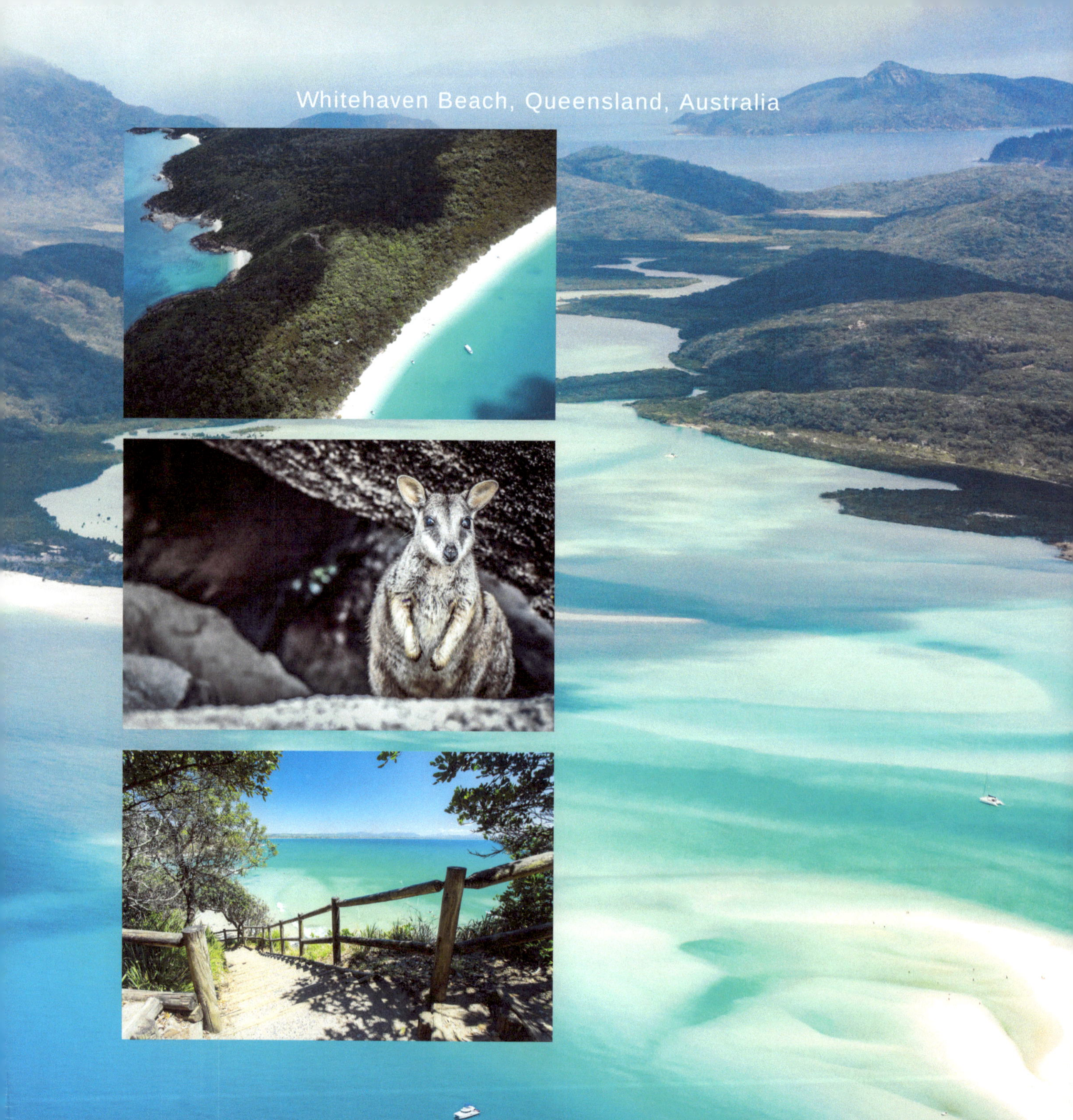
Whitehaven Beach, Queensland, Australia

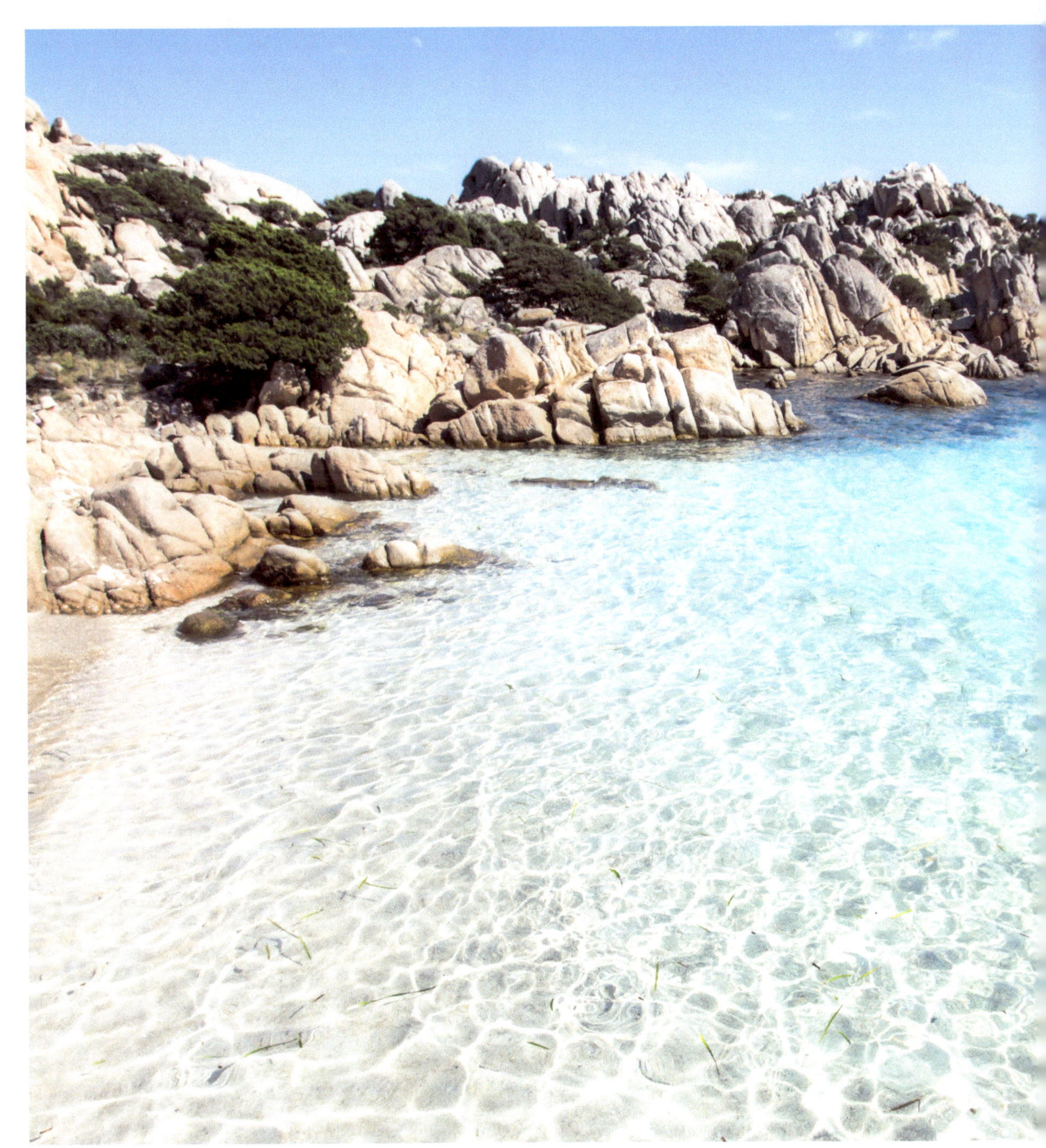

Cala Goloroitze,
Italy

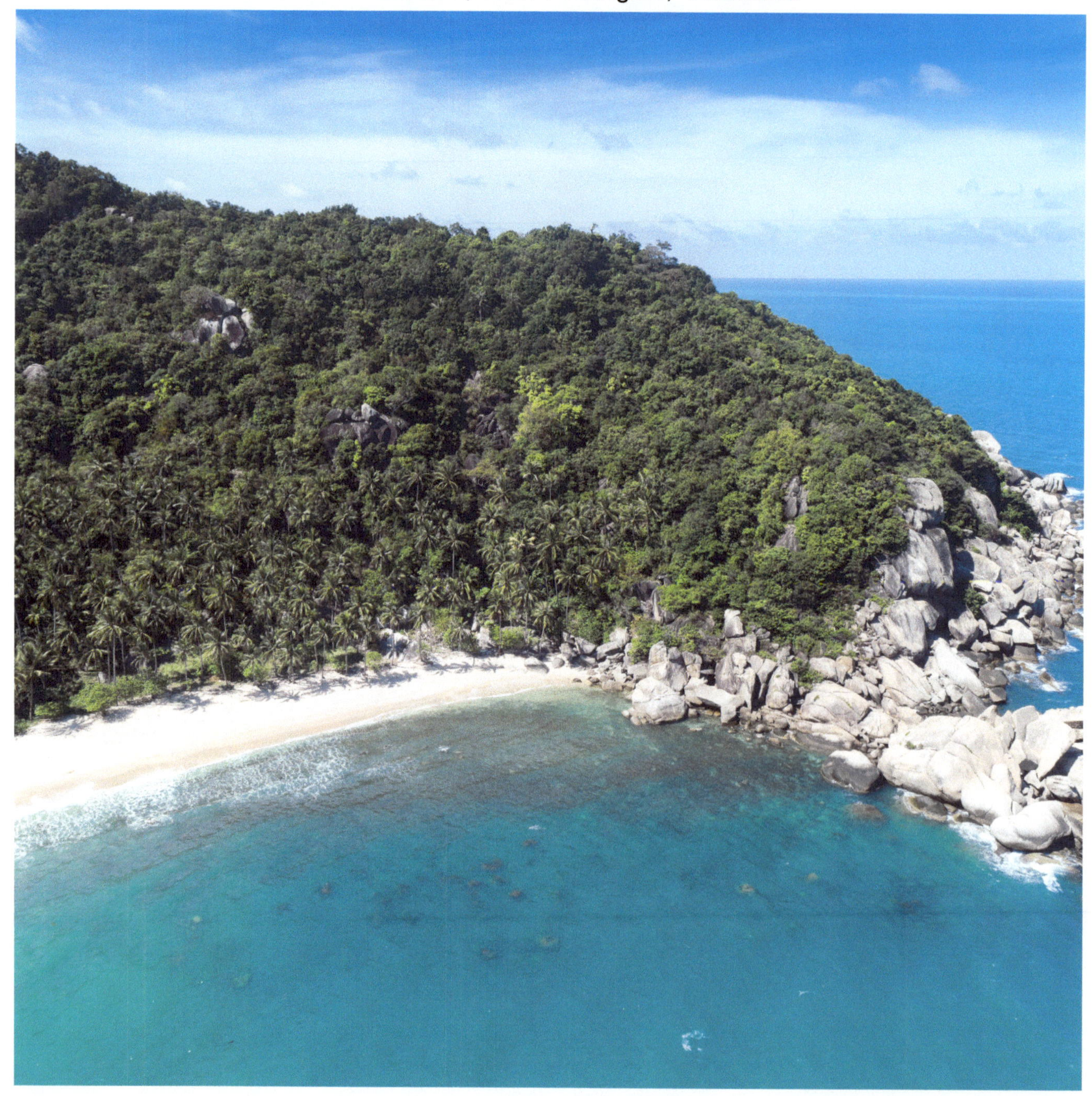

Haad Rin Beach, Koh Phangan, Thailand

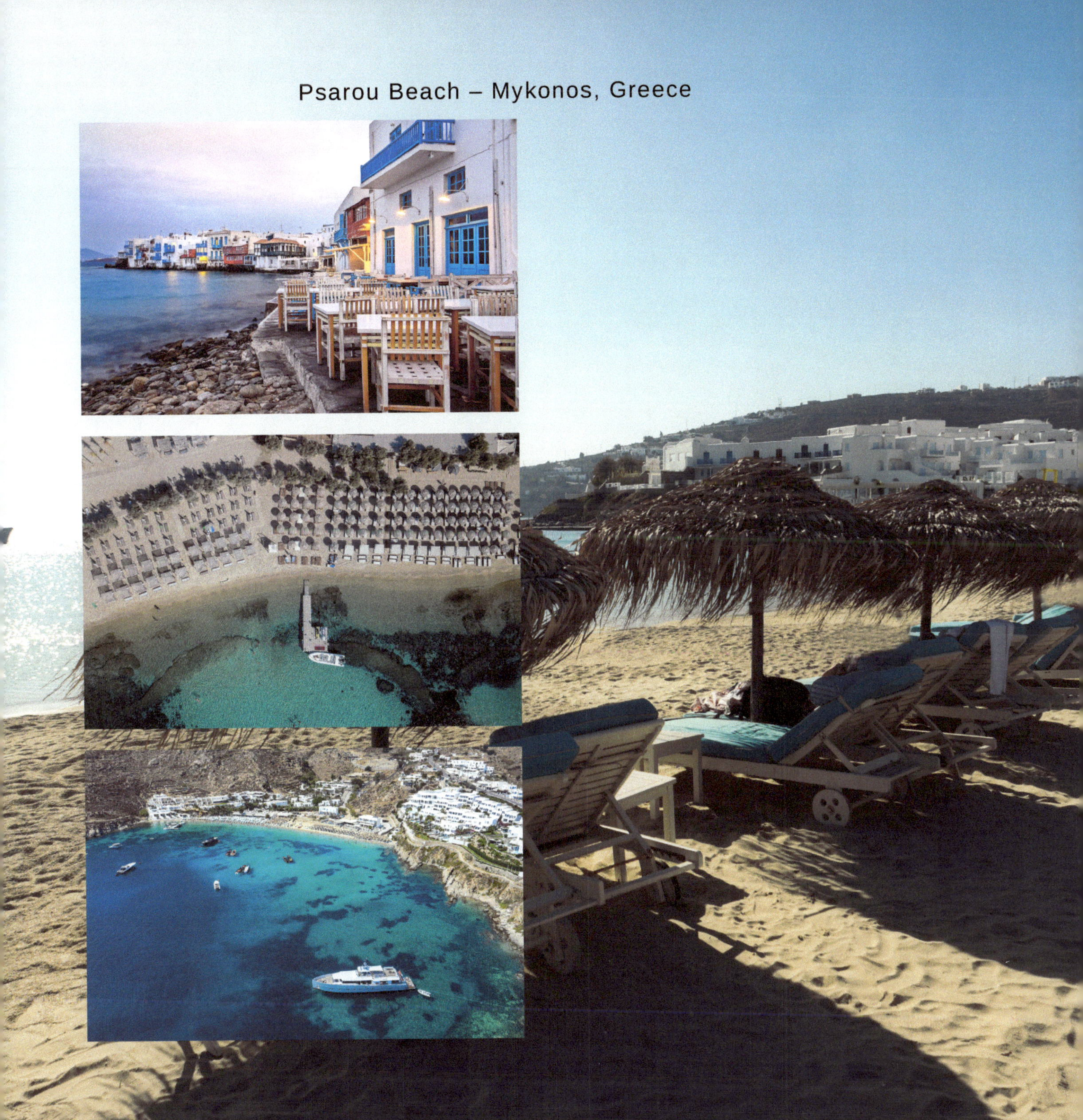

Psarou Beach – Mykonos, Greece

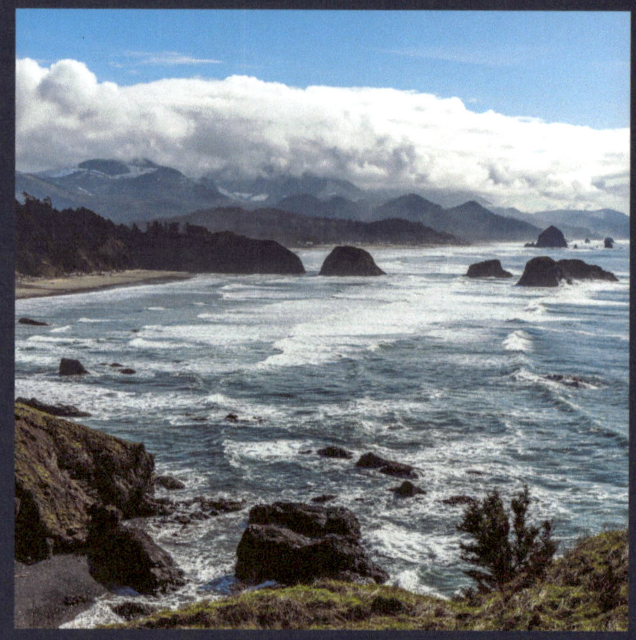

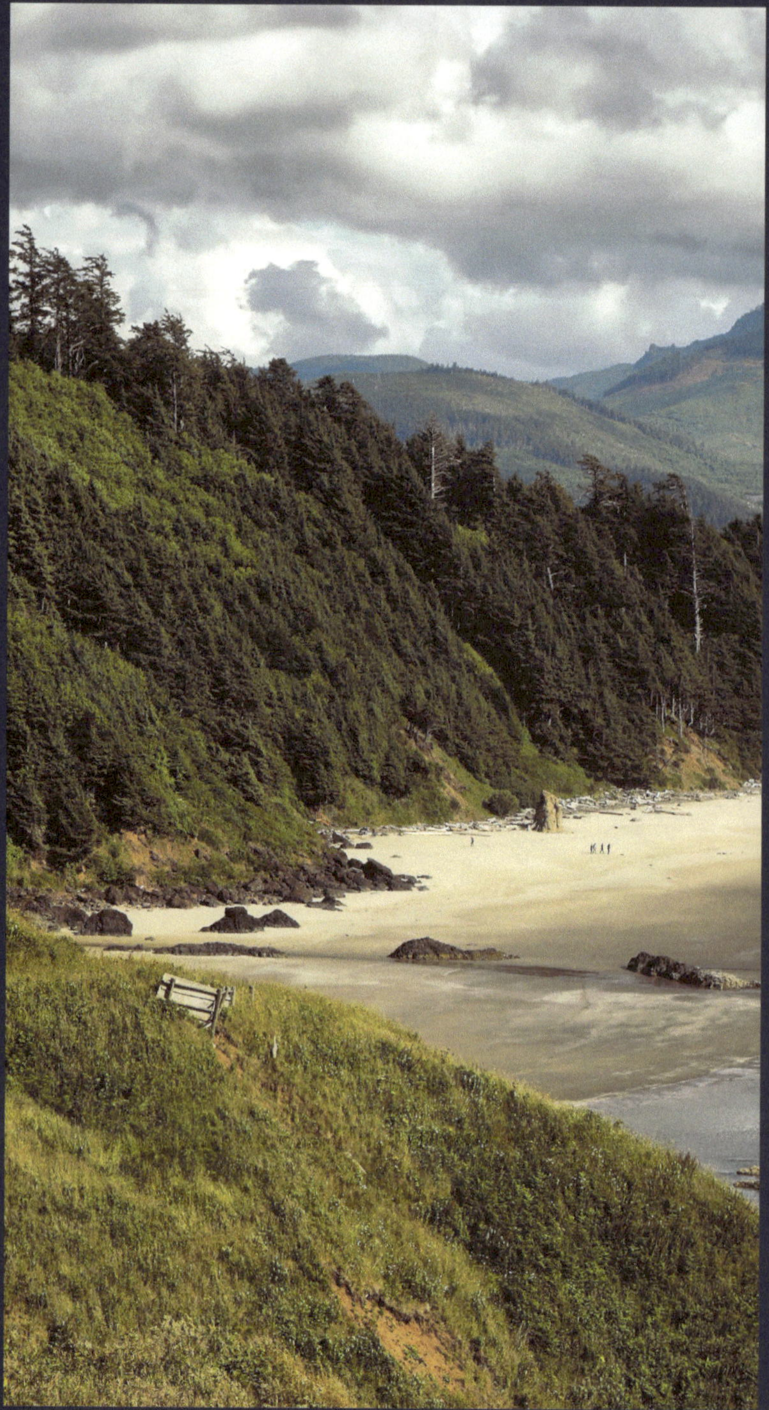

Cannon beach, USA

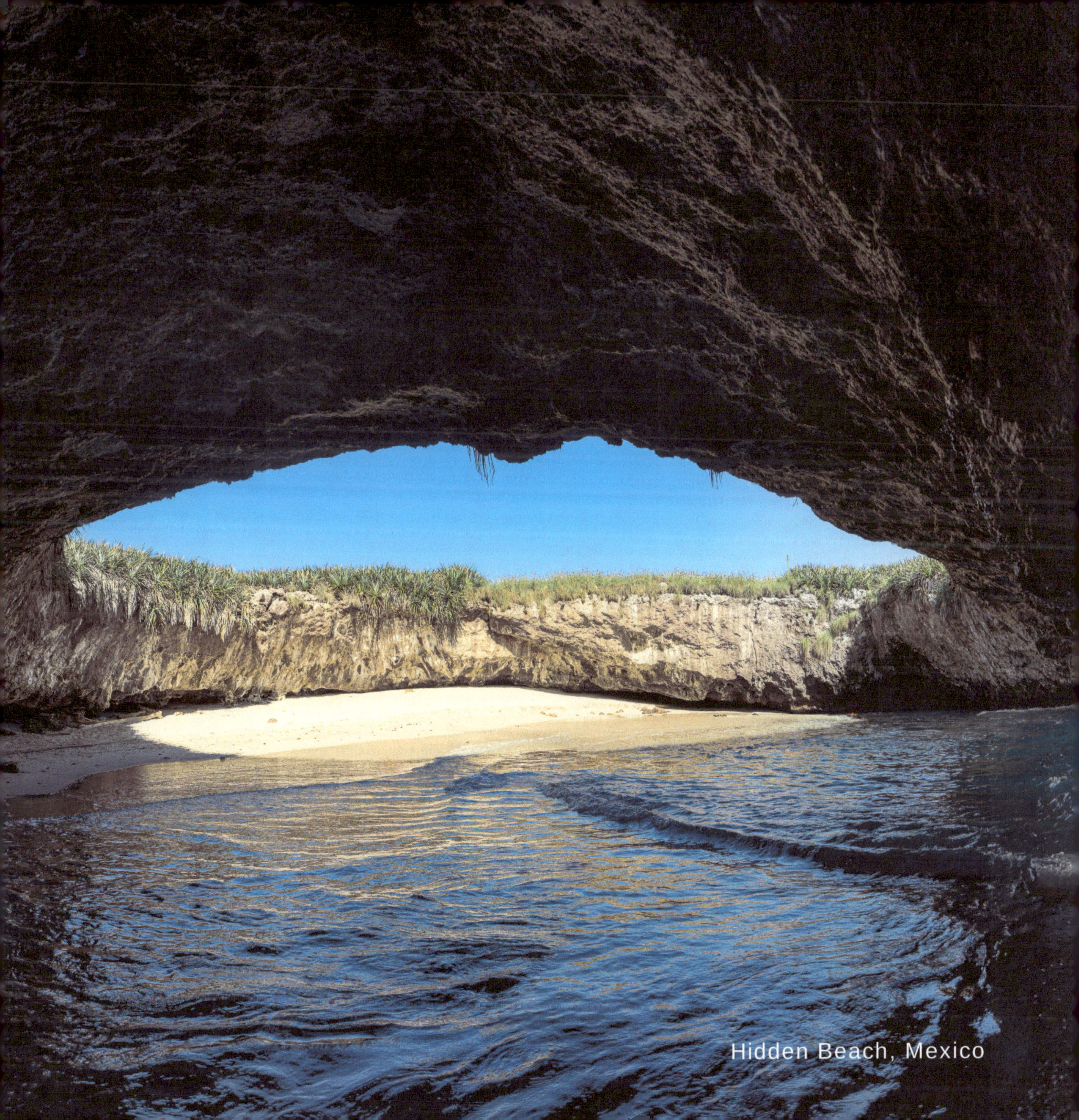
Hidden Beach, Mexico

Beit Yanai, Israel

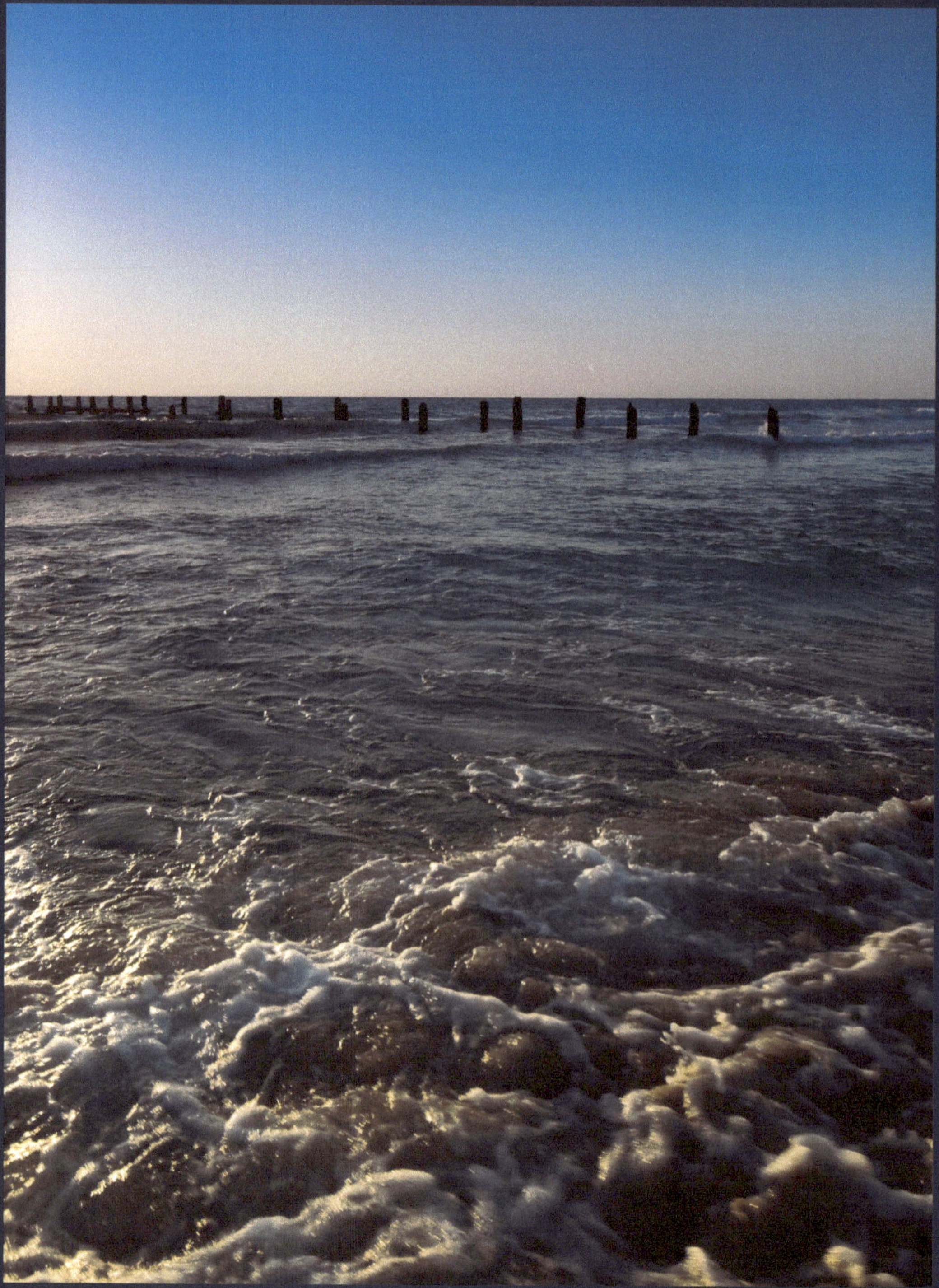

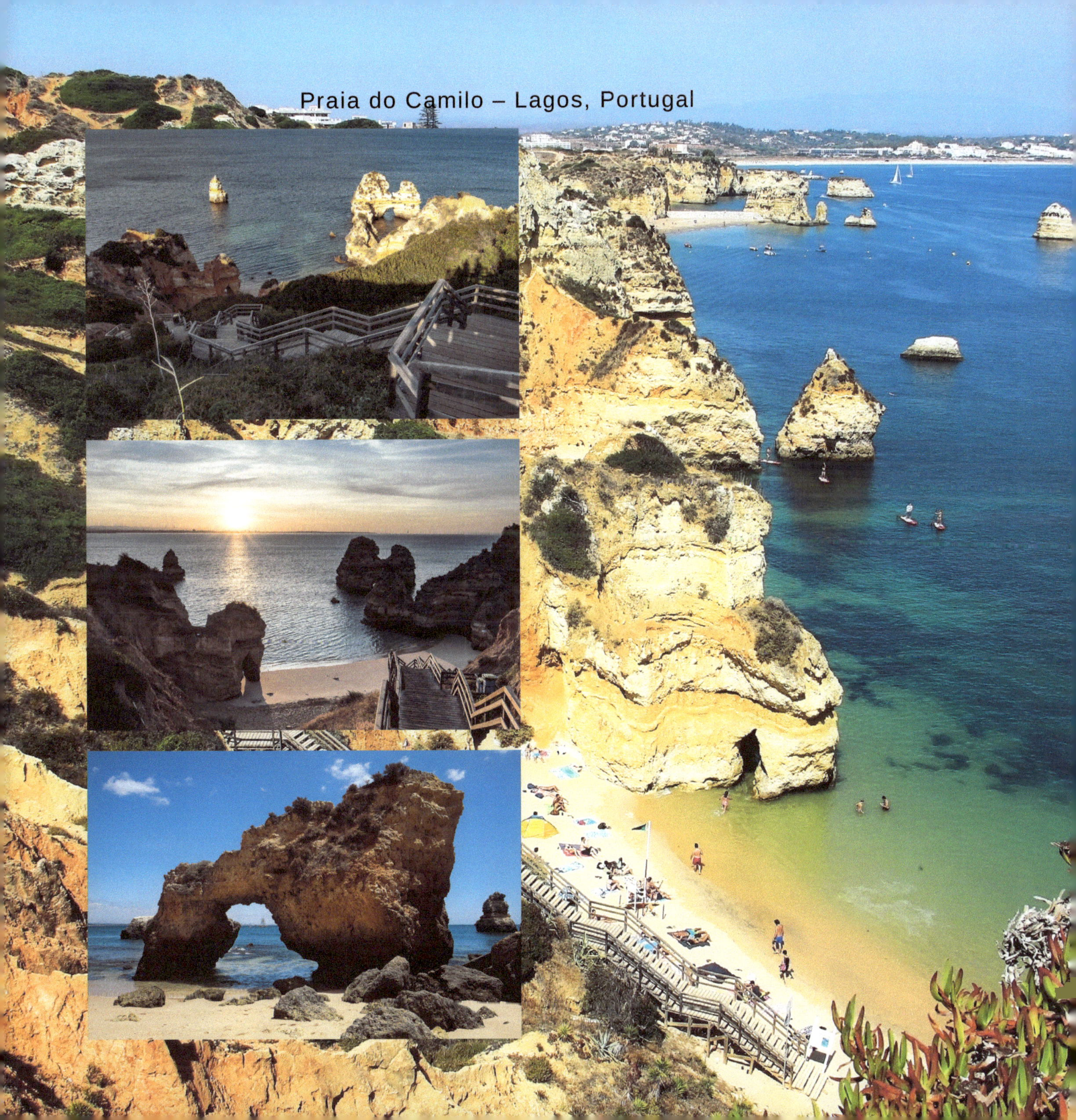

Praia do Camilo – Lagos, Portugal

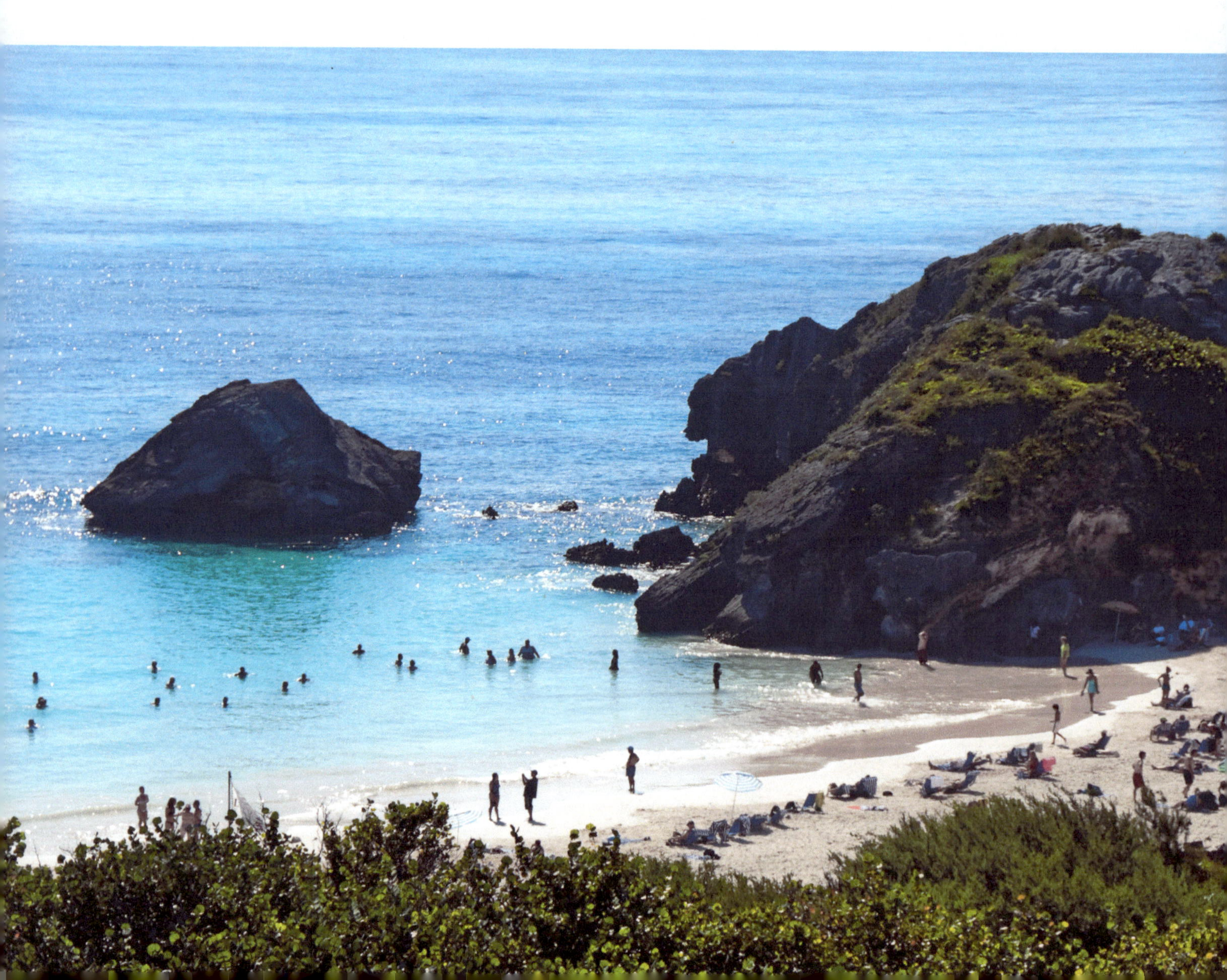

Horseshoe Bay, Bermuda

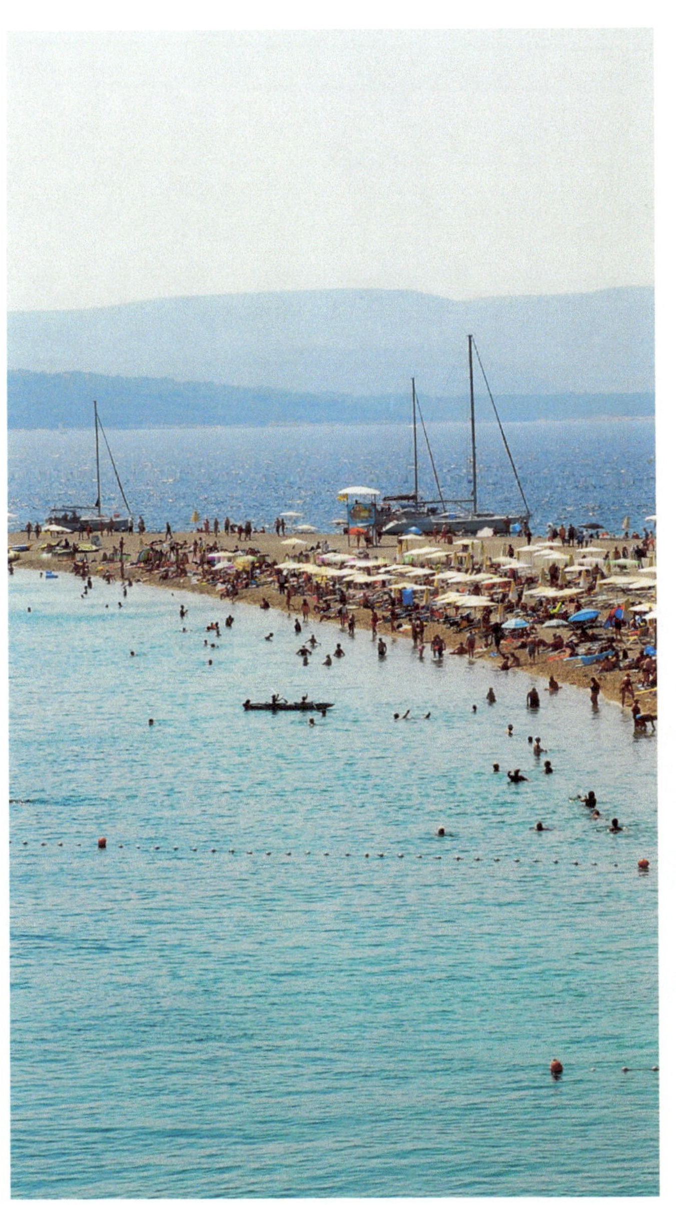

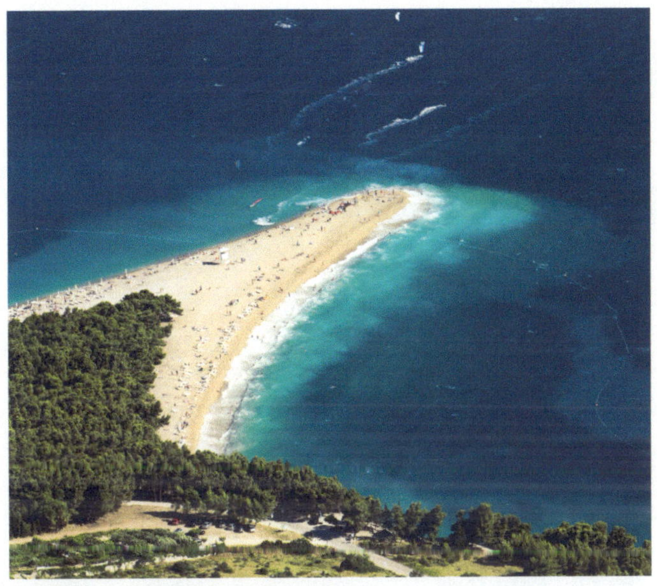

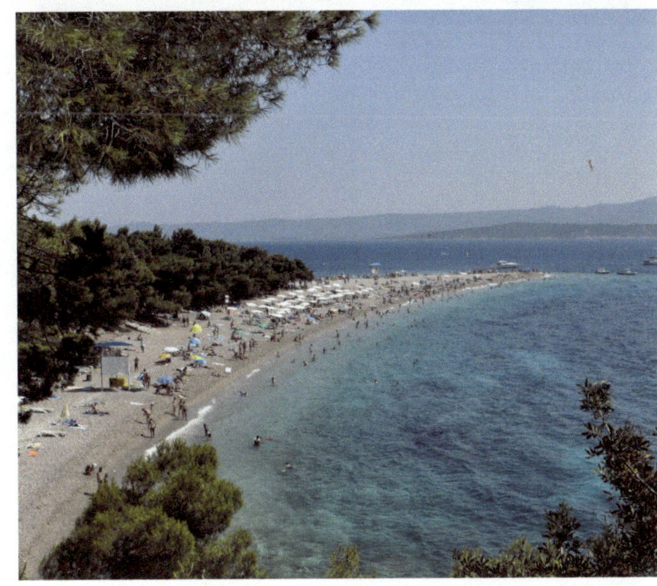

Zlatni Rat, Croatia

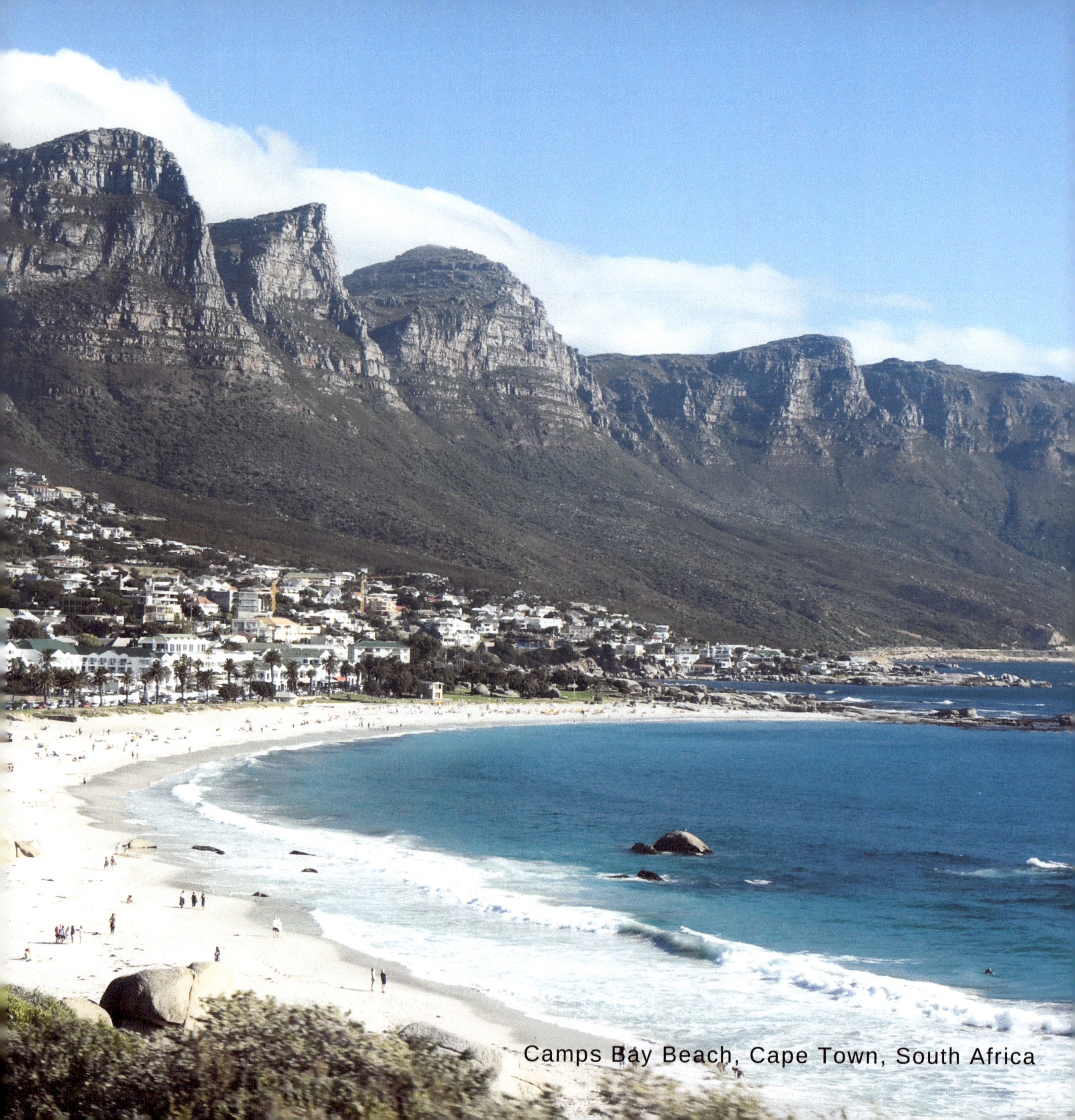

Camps Bay Beach, Cape Town, South Africa

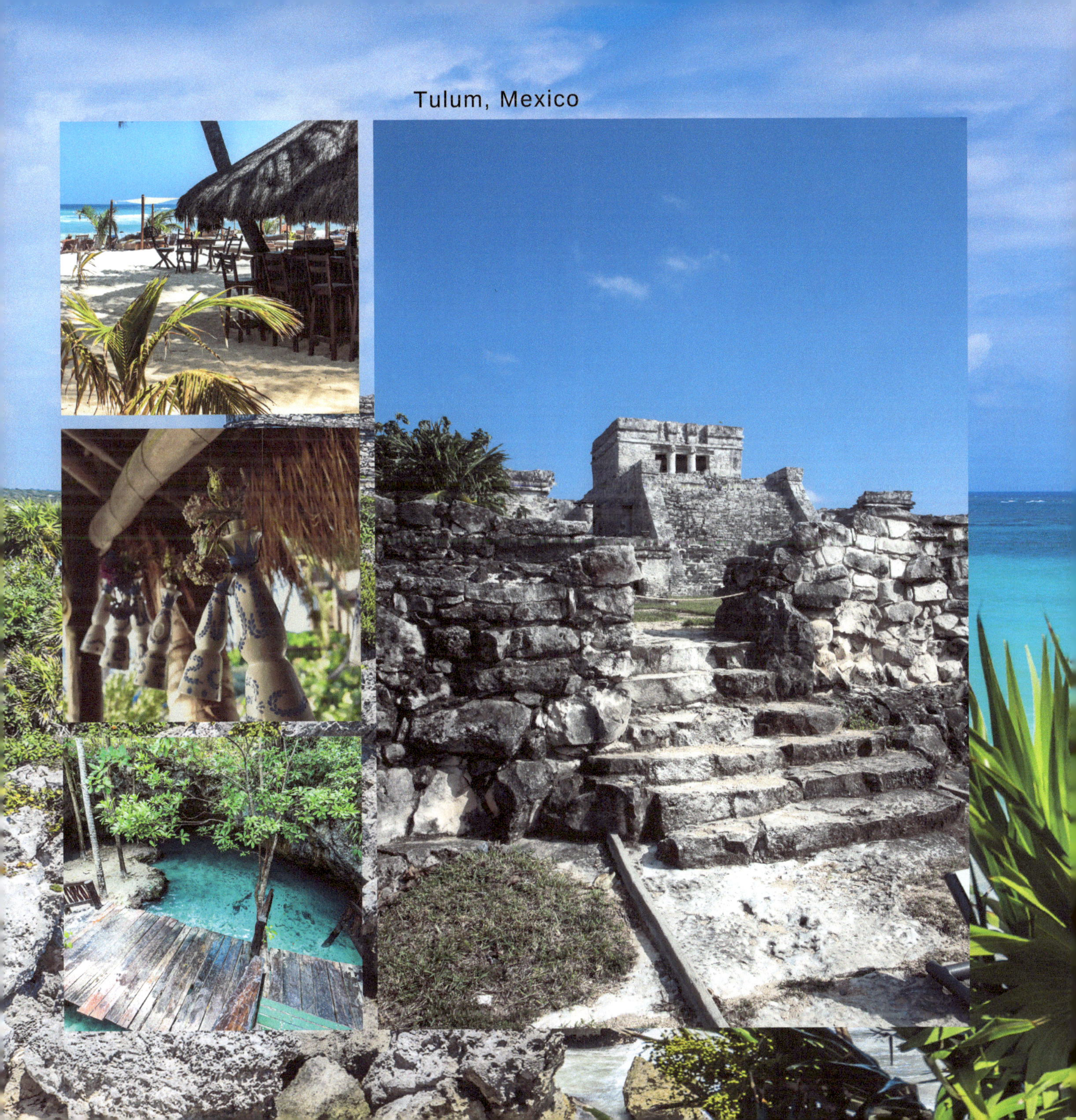

Tulum, Mexico

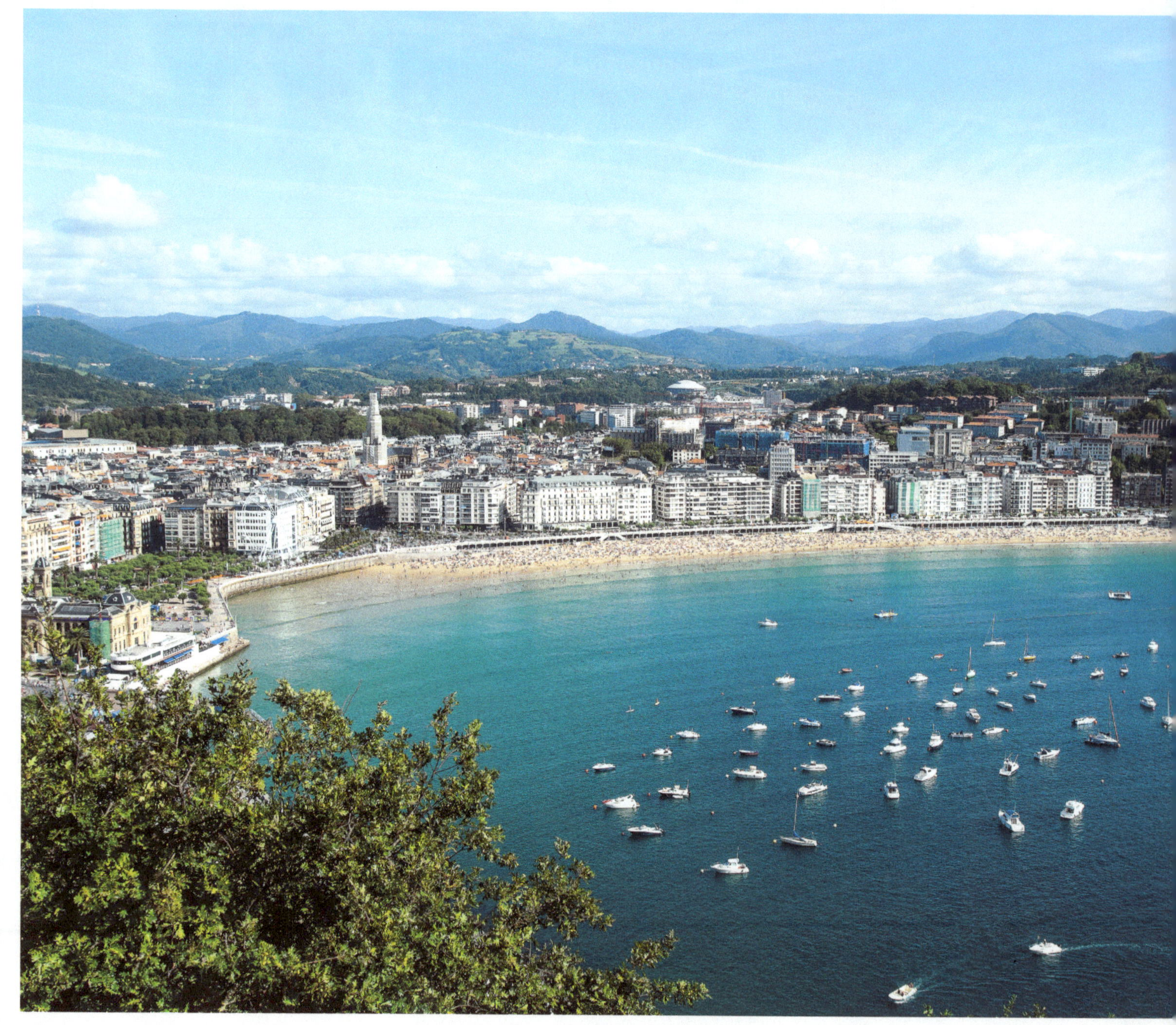

Beach of La Concha

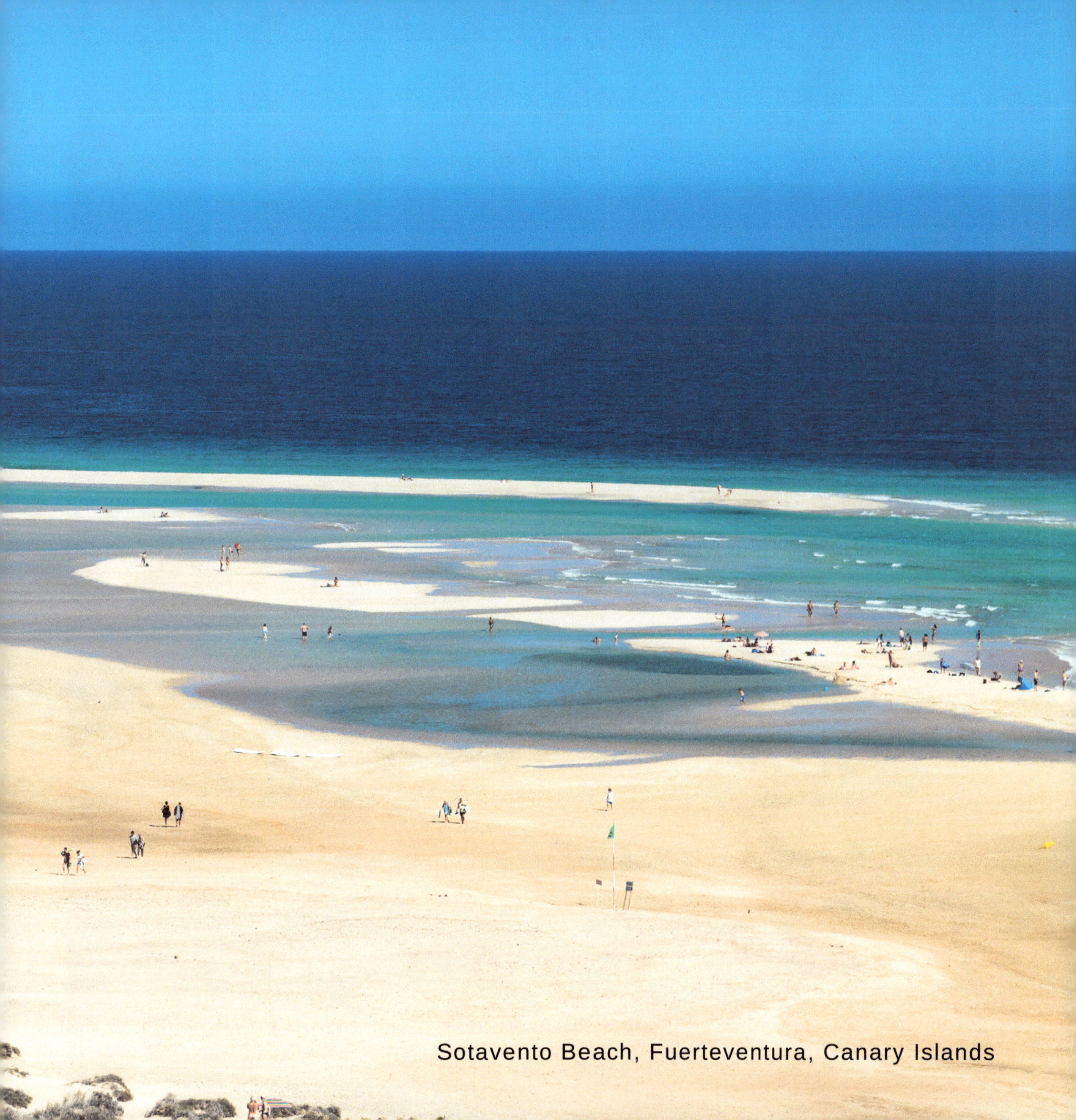

Sotavento Beach, Fuerteventura, Canary Islands

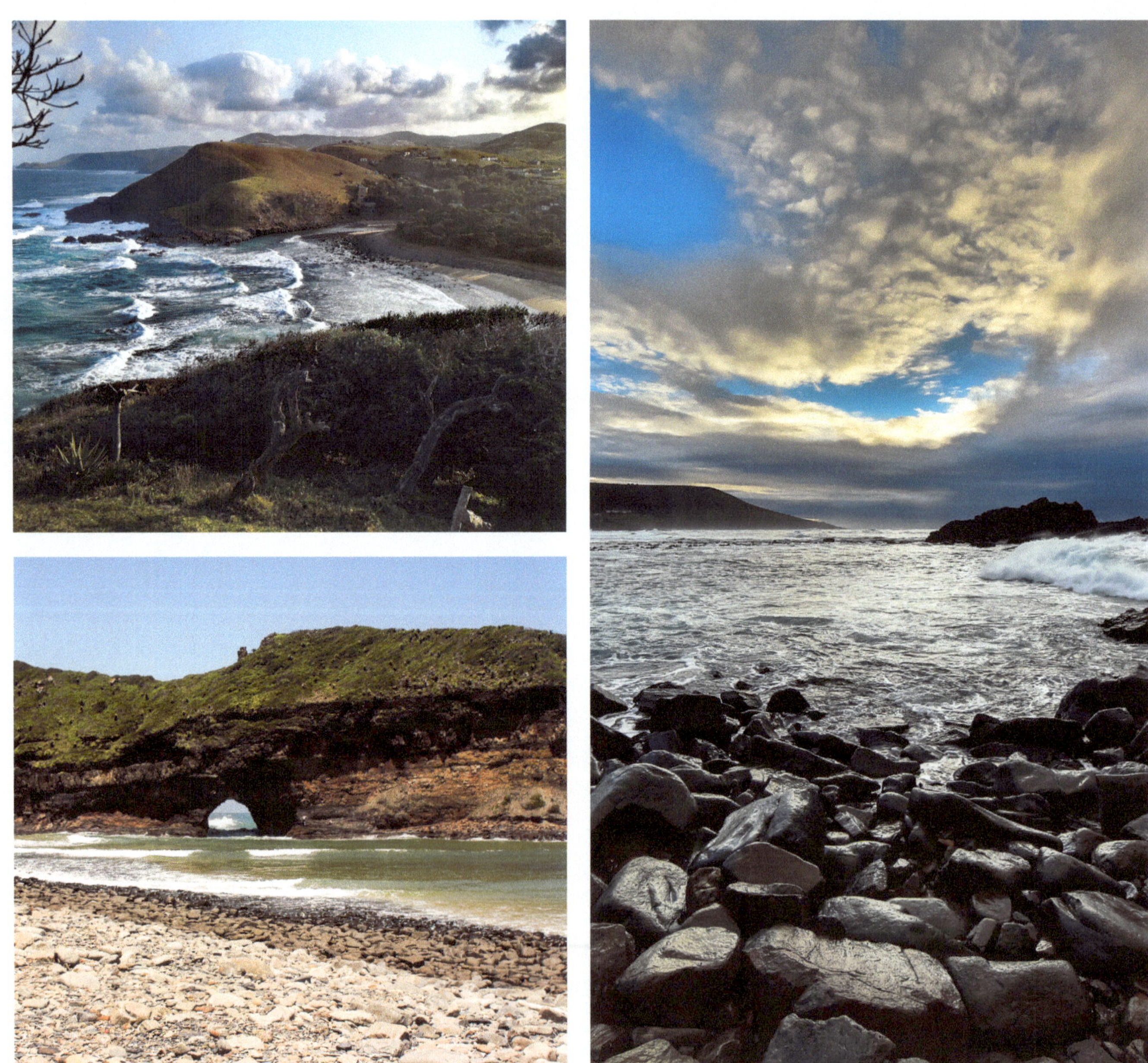

Coffee Bay, South Africa

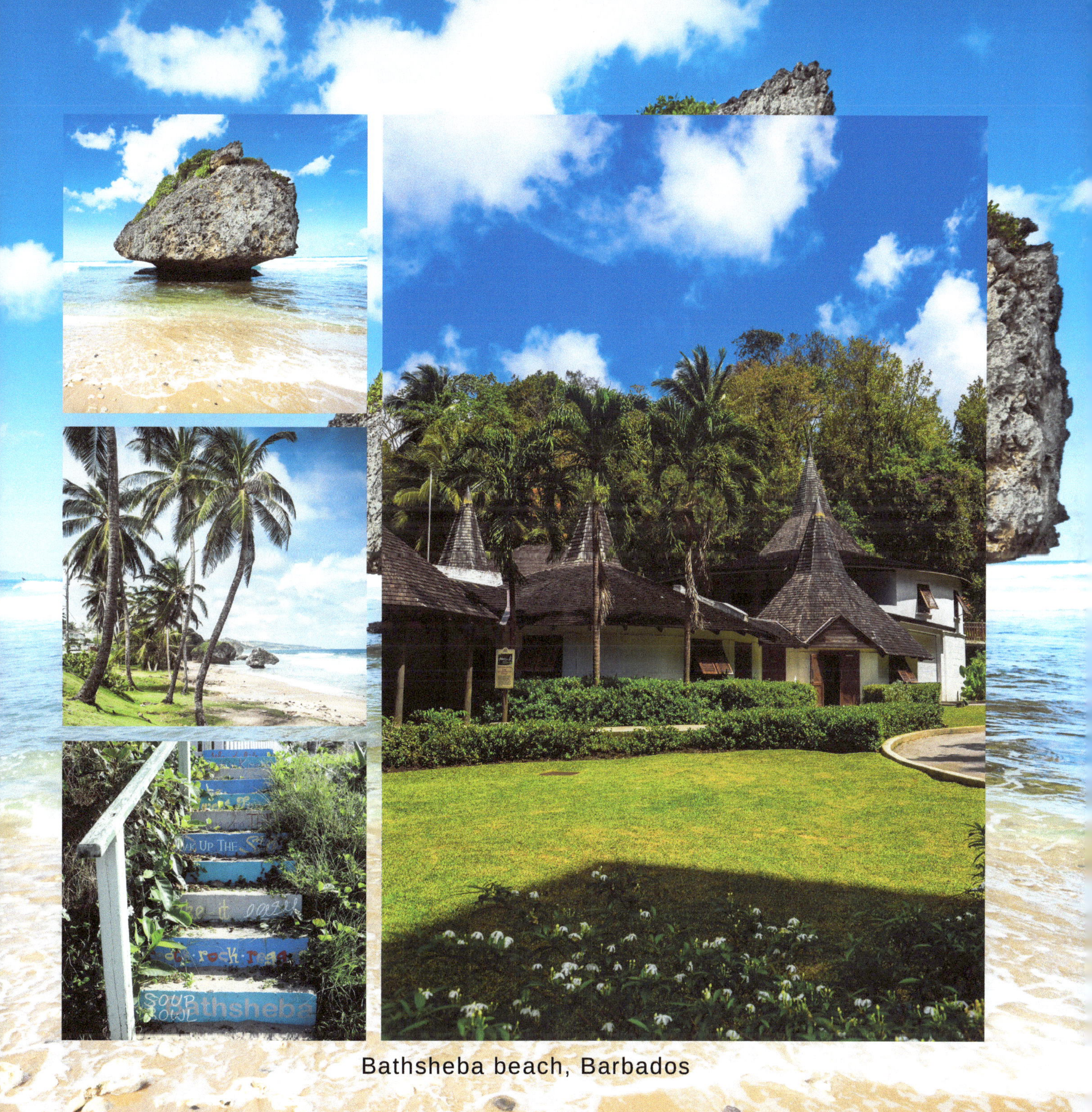

Bathsheba beach, Barbados

www.ingramcontent.com/pod-product-compliance
Lightning Source LLC
LaVergne TN
LVHW070024220726
843527LV00014B/363